# SHELLEY

The uplifting story of a battle
to overcome disfigurement

## Shelley Hull

SHELLEY

Published 2019 by Hornet Books

Text © Shelley Hull

This Work © Hornet Books Ltd

Paperback ISBN 978-0-9957658-5-6

*This book is also available as an ebook*

General Editor: David Roberts
Editor: Elizabeth Badovinac
Proofreader: Suzannah Young

Hornet Books, Ground Floor, 2B Vantage Park,
Washingley Road, Huntingdon, PE29 6SR
www.hornetbooks.com
info@hornetbooks.com

For all the children
and adults
that have a facial deformity.

You are all beautiful

# Foreword

By John L. B. Carter, FRCPS, FRCS, FDSRCS
Oral and Maxillofacial Surgeon, London

Although I only visited Dr. Henderson's clinic at St. Thomas' hospital once, when I was a Senior Registrar at Great Ormond Street [Hospital] where we treated similar cases and at East Grinstead where I worked for his close friend (and fishing companion) Mr. Peter Banks, Derek Henderson was one of several pioneering Oral and Maxillofacial surgeons in England who courageously took the range of skills in our speciality in the 1970s forward, recognising that facial disproportion requires modification of the scaffold of the underlying bone structure as well as the overlying, draping soft tissue.

The concept of a "functional matrix" recognises these complex, inseparable tissue dependencies.

The syndromes which affect facial proportions are many and varied and Shelley's condition of Hemifacial microsomia (HFM) is still extremely uncommon. HFM is, so far as I am aware, unrelated to infection or any other remediable cause. Her detailed reminiscences are a sensitive written record of individual triumph over the trials and tribulations of a challenged life and echo the feelings which many of our courageous patients express.

# Foreword

By Mr. Nayeem Ali, FDSRCS., FRCS (OMFS) Royal
London Hospital

I first met Shelley at The Royal London Hospital with
my then Consultant trainer, John Carter. John had
looked after Shelley when Derek Henderson retired
and I was honoured when John asked me to take
over Shelley's care when he came to retire. Shelley's
journey through the management of her complex
condition had of course been documented in Derek
Henderson's excellent textbook (*A Colour Atlas and
Textbook of Orthognathic Surgery: The Surgery of Facial
Skeletal Deformity*), which I had read as a surgical
trainee and was subsequently given to me by John
Carter.

Hemifacial microsomia is an immensely challenging
condition and rectifying such a complex three-
dimensional hard and soft-tissue abnormality
had only really become possible with advances in
both anaesthesia and surgery that occurred during
Shelley's lifetime. The ability to "borrow" tissue from
other parts of the body and get it to take, function, and
even grow was a milestone that allowed surgeons such

as Derek Henderson and John Carter to treat Shelley and others with her condition. I carried out some refinement procedures for Shelley and marvelled at her tenacity and determination, not only in pursuing her own treatment, but in sharing her experience.

Shelley is a very exacting, attractive woman who takes great pride in her appearance and demonstrates to us all that obstacles in life can be overcome with drive and determination. I am delighted she has chosen to highlight her journey, one she should be immensely proud of.

# "I'm Going to Write a Book!"

I am sitting in a clean, fresh-looking waiting room, ready to be called in for my annual photo shoot. The space is decorated with simple, modern furniture and some standard fashion and lifestyle magazines, but even its cheery ambience can't hold off my slight annoyance.

*I'm fifty-three*, I think to myself, smoothing out an invisible wrinkle on my trousers. *Do they really need another photo?*

The door to my right opens, and I sit up a little straighter.

A woman stands in the doorway, peering through her glasses at a pile of paperwork in her hand. She's wearing a check shirt and some plain trousers, and her thick, dark brown hair is cut short at her collar, giving her the appearance of a receptionist. An identity badge hangs from her neck, but the only text I can make out is "Medical Illustration Department".

After what seems like an eternity, her eyes flick up from the paperwork to find me. "Shelley Hull?"

"That's me," I say, and stand up to hand her

the flimsy piece of paper I've just received from the outpatients department.

She glances down at the crumpled sheet and nods. "Follow me, please."

We walk through the little hallway into the photo shoot room. It's large compared to the tiny waiting room, with spotlights in every corner. I sit down in the big, black leather chair in the centre of the room, already anticipating the heat of the lights focused on my face. I grin a little to myself, feeling like I'm centre stage or in an interrogation room. And it's not even *Mastermind*!

The woman sets to sorting out the equipment in preparation for the shoot, and I realise she's actually the photographer for the day. She balances her glasses on her nose as she looks at the outpatient information again. "So, you're coming in for an operation on your face?" she asks, setting the paper on a nearby table as she appraises my face with a soft frown. She reaches up and pats her cheek. "I can see you must be wanting to get that sorted."

"Oh, no—I've had all my operations," I say. "This is just an update of the photographs."

She's already across the room, adjusting a spotlight. "Mhm. Don't you worry, I'm sure the doctors will be able to sort it out for you."

I glance over at her, too surprised to say anything else. *Did you even listen to what I just said?*

"Are you in pain?" she asks, completely oblivious.

*The only thing that's painful is this conversation,* I think, but try to muster up a smile that she probably won't even notice. "No."

When she finishes adjusting the lights and screens, the photo shoot begins and ends in a blur. Beyond a few instructions, we remain civil to each other. Still, I can't help but think that if I'd been anyone else, her assumptions and comments probably would've offended me.

She powers down the lights and steps out from behind the camera, giving me a smile. "All finished. Let me just finish your paperwork and then I'll walk you out."

I bite my lip as she scribbles down some information, unsettled. What if she *had* said something about someone else's face? What if she had said something like that to me when I was a child, vulnerable and self-conscious? "You know, I had a lot of operations as a child and teenager," I blurt out. "This is as good as it gets."

Her hand freezes above the paperwork as she looks at me, eyebrows raised. "Oh?"

I nod, giving her a bit more history about all the surgery I endured growing up. The more I speak, the more interested she becomes. By the end, she's pulled up a chair.

"Can you tell me more?" she asks, as I finish my story. Her eyes have softened, giving me a look that I recognise as one of compassion—but more so of genuine curiosity. She doesn't seem to be in any hurry, and I know she's probably rethinking her comments about my face.

Feeling a little lighter, I explain more about what happened to me, a story that I've told before but one that never seems to lose its impact. She asks me if it would be alright for her to browse through my medical notes on file when she has time. Of course, I agree. I always do.

"You should really write a book about your journey," she finally says, chewing thoughtfully on the tip of her glasses. "I think people would really find it interesting, and helpful."

I give her a polite grin. *Yeah, right.* "Yeah, maybe."

***

# *"You should really write a book"*

The photographer at the hospital had planted a seed, one I couldn't stop thinking about for the next couple of weeks. Slowly, her kind words morphed in my mind, taking root and growing into a tangible, internalised vision:

You should *really write a book.*

I should *really write a book.*

Could I actually do it? I'd never really thought about it before. I'm not much of a reader, and apart from occasionally making it through short stories in magazines, my mind tends to wander off after even the first few pages. I was used to writing a note, a Post-It memo, even the odd email to a company—but a book? The thought of me writing anything longer than a page or two sounded like quite a challenge, to say the least.

And while the seed had been planted, there was also a question I'd yet to answer: *How? How* would I write down my experiences and tell others of my journey? Where would I begin? How would I start, where would I put the paragraphs, the timeline—how could I break it into segmented parts of my life? Was it like a puzzle? Did I start from the beginning? Or should

I start at the end and work back? (Oh, and when I say "end", I mean present day—I'm not dead yet!)

The first name that came to mind was Dr. Derek Henderson, one of my old primary surgeons. In addition to knowing my case the best, Dr. Henderson had been with me since nearly the beginning. He had more information on my situation than even I knew, and I knew his help would be invaluable. Even more importantly, I felt the need to use this opportunity to write to him, making up my mind to let him know that I was going to write a book and tell the world how grateful and blessed I was that he had changed my life through the surgeries he'd performed.

Writing to him, I knew, was long overdue. I'd contacted him several years ago to see if he was still practising, wanting to discuss further treatment and obtain a referral for another maxillofacial surgeon. But since then, I hadn't bothered to check in—and he had long since retired. I also had no idea where to contact him, since he'd run a practice in France but had retired in England.

Setting to work trying to discover his new address, I sifted through all my old paperwork. Finding no recent information, I took to the Internet and there came across the news that Dr. Henderson had passed away.

Eyes widening, I double-checked to make sure I was reading about the right Derek Henderson.

Unfortunately, I was.

Grief and shock ran through me as I sat back in my chair, trying to process my emotions. I was sad for his family and their loss, but the knowledge that he'd passed away also hit me hard. This fascinating, pioneering surgeon, who had been in my life from a very young age, had left this earth. The one person who knew all about my rare condition, who could help if there was an infection or query with my procedures, who could refer me to dentists and oral surgeons, was no longer available to contact.

It was a moment of feeling terrified and alone all at once. But as I absorbed the sad news, the seed within my mind began to grow.

Dr. Derek Henderson's remarkable work changed my life. He had watched me grow from a timid young girl into a survivor, and had been there through some of my darkest times. The world needed to know what he'd done, and I was—I am—the only person who could tell this story.

It was on this premise that I began to remember. To relive. To write. And I knew just where to begin.

I AM *going to write a book.*

***

Right now, I'm asking myself this question: Who would really want to read about me? I know that's not the typical way to start off an autobiography, but the fact is, I don't want to bore you with a book about "Me, Myself and I".

There are plenty of people out there from all walks of life with some amazing and wonderful stories to tell. Lots of famous people write about their lives in autobiographies. It's interesting to read about their personal lives, away from what we seem to see them as in the public eye. There are autobiographies about wars, about families getting divided up during evacuations. There are books about sad or even cruel upbringings. There are stories of heartbreak, struggle, and determination in the face of adversity.

Me? Who am I? I'm just an ordinary person who had a fair amount of operations in my younger years. That's it. That's what I want to tell you about.

But, as you may imagine, it's a little more than just that.

*Shelley* is my story of growing up as a young girl with facial disfigurement, daring to wish that one day—some day—I'd live a normal life and fit in. It records the journey of a timid, shy child with no self-confidence or worth through the world of modern medicine and maxillofacial surgery, with setbacks around every corner, a child who blossomed into a confident survivor who seeks to inspire others with a story of hardship, hope, and perspective. It is the record of remarkable medical surgeries and the emotional and mental factors that accompany childhood disfigurement and treatment.

And, perhaps most importantly, it details the transformation of my life—not only physically, but emotionally too—through the work of family, friends, medical personnel, and doctors like Dr. Derek Henderson, a pioneering oral and maxillofacial surgeon.

Yes, I am just an *ordinary* person... and I take great pride in saying that, because I've fought to be "ordinary" for most of my life! My ascent into "ordinary" and "normal" was not just a physical one, either. I've learnt throughout the years that surgery can only go so far; without grit, confidence, and self-love, transformation cannot occur.

You might be thinking, *why now?* Why share this story in my early fifties? Why has it taken me this long to write my story when most of my changes happened years ago?

First, the consequences and scars of the

bullying, self-loathing, and fear I experienced in my youth have been far-reaching and long-lasting. But I have finally reached an age where I have come to terms with being able to write publicly about my feelings and the way I looked when I was younger— along with all the adversities and challenges I had to overcome. I no longer cringe at the thought of my childhood photo being published for everyone to see. (Well, maybe a little—but a reminder or two of reality puts me back on track.)

Second, I have a wonderful husband and three wonderful sons, all of whom are fully supportive of me writing this book. I needed their reassurance and approval, as I wouldn't want to write a story that I felt could affect their feelings too. My heartfelt thanks goes to all of them for being understanding and for encouraging me throughout this process.

With this foundation, my hope for you, reader, is that you will be interested, and maybe even a little inspired, by my story. If there is one message I'd like you to take from this book, it is that we all go from face to face—whether physically as I did, mentally, emotionally, or spiritually—as we progress in our lives. But transformation, new "faces" that we build for ourselves or others build for us, takes perseverance, support, compassion, and understanding, even if we must endure a number of setbacks and challenges in the process. Most of all, this journey takes love, both from others and within ourselves.

That doesn't make transformation easy. But it does make it totally worth it in the end.

**Shelley Hull**

CHAPTER 1

# "There's just something not quite right"

My story begins on the day I came into the world: December 16, 1962. It was a Sunday and I was born at home, arriving nine days earlier than expected. My due date should have been December 25, but to this day I thank my lucky stars I didn't have a birthday and Christmas all on one day. Well done, Mum.

Two days before I was born, an intense fog settled over London. The bad weather prevented any taxis or buses from running, and my father was at work, driving his long-distance lorry, so my mother found herself having to walk from work in Central London to our home in Hackney. The trip took about four hours, as she stopped and rested at each corner, fighting the weather and her pregnancy all at once.

The next day, my father arrived home. On Sunday, my mother felt unwell and went to lie down on the bed. She dozed off for a while, then woke up with the sudden urge to give birth—in her words, I "just popped out"!

My father didn't really have a clue what to do, so he ran to a neighbour's house, where a registered nurse lived. Luckily, she was home and came over to attend to my mother and me. As the nurse cleaned me up, my mother saw her frown.

"There's just something not quite right," our neighbour said, peering down at me through narrowed eyes. She said she noticed some abnormalities on my face, much to the alarm of my mother.

They both, along with my father, realised that my ears weren't quite identical—besides them sticking out and being different in size, I seemed to have a third, underformed ear in front of my left one.

"Don't worry too much about it," our neighbour eventually reassured my parents. "It can be corrected later, with a doctor."

The next couple of weeks seemed to fly by. My mum was recovering well from giving birth to me, following the usual post-pregnancy schedule of staying in bed for the first two weeks. That was normal in those days, since home births were common. Despite the rest period, Mum had her hands full and had to acclimatise herself to a new routine, especially since she was now raising me along with my brother, who was two years older than me and kept everybody in the house busy.

Christmas and the New Year passed, and any thoughts of bringing me to the doctor to be examined quickly dissipated as the weather started to change for the worse. It became extremely cold and started to blizzard, the snow coming in full and thick. The first four inches arrived on Boxing Day, then another ten inches covered London on the night of December 29. Later, it'd be referred to as the Big Freeze of 1963, where temperatures were continuously below freezing and it snowed for twenty-one days in January and twenty days in February.

Because of the weather, people hardly ventured from their houses. Public transport was shut down, and businesses suffered. Residents had a hard time getting to and from work, and even my mother could not get me to the local welfare clinic for weighing and regular check-ups.

During the early weeks of the New Year and the bad weather, my father was away working. As he was a long-distance lorry driver, his job kept him away from home for days at a time. My mum stayed with my brother and me, keeping the house as warm as she could—especially with a newborn baby in the house.

Like many newborns, I slept many hours after feeds—I suppose they call it the "growing time". But one day, my mum came into the bedroom to check on me in my cot to find my skin looking pale, almost grey. Panicking, she tried to wake me.

I remained asleep, unresponsive. It was a mother's worst nightmare.

Fearing for my life, my mum ran next door to the neighbour's, screaming: "Help me! I think my baby is dead!"

At those words, her neighbour rushed in and picked me up, wrapping me in a blanket and calling an ambulance. This took us to Queen Elizabeth Hospital, in Hackney, London.

***

The paramedics whisked me into the Baby Care Unit at the hospital and placed me in an incubator. They attached tubes, wires, and oxygen where they could, and also linked me up to monitors. Later, my mum would tell me that the incubator was a large, glasslike dome. The only way doctors and nurses could touch me was with white gloves attached to the glass wall, preventing any germs from coming in or going out.

Worried about me and frightened that I

wouldn't survive, my mother used the public phone at the hospital to contact my dad's workplace. She informed them of the situation, hoping they'd be able to relay the information to my dad once he returned to the yard. His usual journeys were to and from Scotland, which would take some days to complete. And, thanks to the awful weather, his speedy return was uncertain at best. My mum would have to face these pivotal first days alone, her youngest child barely clinging to life.

The next few hours in hospital went by agonizingly slowly, until my mum was called into a room and given the bad news. I was still very weak and generally unresponsive. The medical staff also told my mum that I was underweight for my age, which she'd been unable to have checked at the clinic because of the bad weather. To top it all off, visiting hours were almost over. It was time for her to go.

As a parent myself, I cannot begin to imagine the anguish my mum was going through, not knowing what was to be the outcome. Back in those days, parents were not allowed to stay with their children on the ward. Visiting hours were very strict. Mum had no choice but to leave me in the hospital and go home, to return the following day and discover if I'd survived the night.

One day turned into several, and several days

turned into weeks. My mum—and my dad, when he could—visited every day, watching me from behind the clear, sterile glass of my incubator. After a few weeks, the attending physicians confirmed that I was not responding to the drugs that were being administered to me intravenously. I was slowly deteriorating.

"You should prepare yourselves for the worst," a doctor grimly told my parents. "We're unable to do anything further for your baby."

A few more weeks went on, and upon advice from the staff at the hospital, a hospital priest was summoned to perform Last Rites. My family began to lose all hope, along with my entire extended family. Later, my aunt would recall my dad's face and reactions. He kept saying: "My baby is going to die," as if he was preparing himself every minute. It didn't help that he had to continue working for the family, to keep the money coming in. The stress was mounting on everyone, and every day they were told I was one step closer to death. Everyone assumed it'd just be a matter of time.

The days continued to drag on with no change in my condition. The snow, though easing off a little, made it hard for my family to visit me in hospital. The doctors, still pessimistic about what my outcome would be, continued to observe me. After a few more weeks, they told my parents that they were amazed to see I had not deteriorated any further. Their surprise only deepened when I slowly started to pick up. My colour started to return, and I slowly began to increase in weight. Each day, I grew stronger and stronger.

That didn't mean my time at the hospital was over, however. In fact, it was far from done.

\*\*\*

Shortly after I began to recover, the doctors requested a meeting to discuss my progress with my parents. My mum and dad arrived during visiting hours as usual, and sat down with a physician to hear what he had to say.

"We've run a series of tests," the doctor said, "and we've discovered some abnormalities. We've never come across a baby with a condition like this before."

My parents, shocked at the news, inquired further. While they'd clearly noticed the differences in my ears and the extra ear I had on the left side of my face, they hadn't expected other abnormalities. The doctor explained that, apart from the obvious, I also had a dermoid cyst on the pupil of my right eye, which was still growing and would affect the sight in my eye. No one had noticed it at first, since I'd slept so much after I was born.

There was also the issue of a heart murmur the doctors had discovered, but that wasn't all. My face was additionally underdeveloped on the right side, making one side of my face look much smaller than the other.

"But how did this happen?" my mother asked, as baffled as my father.

"Your guess is as good as mine," the doctor replied with a helpless shrug. "Did you take the drug Thalidomide for morning sickness during your pregnancy?"

My mum replied that she hadn't, which led to another series of questions. Eventually, she mentioned that while she was pregnant, she'd been working in an office in London. One of her work colleagues had gone off sick from work with Rubella (German measles). She herself hadn't got ill or left work, but after some discussion with his colleagues, the doctor came to the conclusion that my mum had been a carrier of the disease and that the virus had got into her baby: me.

My parents were devastated. Questions raced through my mum's mind over and over. Why hadn't she realised? Should she have known? Why hadn't she caught the measles instead of her baby? But despite her grief and regrets, speaking to the doctor made one thing clear: my parents had a baby with abnormalities, and something needed to be done as soon as possible.

"We've never treated a child with this condition before," the doctor reiterated once my parents had absorbed the news. "We're going to refer her to specialist care at the John Radcliffe Hospital in Oxford."

Little did my parents know, this would be the start of a long, seemingly endless journey into modern medicine.

CHAPTER 2

# "He had no arms or legs, but was able to turn the pages with his tongue"

My parents travelled the long distance from London to Oxford, a trip that took hours to reach by car in 1963. I was to see a surgeon, Gavin Livingstone, who was an ear, nose and throat specialist. He had a particular interest in children with abnormalities and was very keen to examine my case.

After a few appointments and tests, Dr. Livingstone explained to my parents that I had no hearing in either ear. In fact, my inner ear canals were not fully formed. The cyst on my pupil was also an area of concern, and needed to be removed right away—before it grew to cover my pupil entirely and caused me to lose my sight completely in that eye.

Everyone sprang into action after that, drawing up plans and procedures for the operations I needed to have on my eye and ears. By the time I was nine months old, everything was prepared. I was admitted to John Radcliffe Hospital, where I'd undergo the complex operations. They were not only going to be lengthy, they would also be difficult due to the rarity of the situation. And, of course, I'd be in this hospital for some months to recuperate.

Soon after being admitted, the growth was removed from my eye. A few weeks later, surgery was done to my ears to improve my hearing. Plastic implants were placed in my left ear to replace structures that were missing, and for the right ear, surgeons drilled a hole through my ear canal to help my inner ear functions, which were also underdeveloped.

Like at Queen Elizabeth Hospital, visiting hours at John Radcliffe Hospital were strict, and the long distance between Oxford and London made it difficult for my parents to visit during the week. They made time to visit over the weekend, though my dad was often away for work so he could continue to provide for our family.

The weekends themselves became a ritual. My older brother would go and stay with my nan and grandad, while Mum and Dad would make the journey to Oxford by car to visit me.

They would stay overnight in a local hotel so they could visit again on Sunday before the long journey home. This would continue for months as I stayed in the hospital to heal.

*** 

Life in the hospital wasn't so bad, especially since I was young and hardly knew anything different. While I was there, I learnt to walk, speak my first words, and eat with a knife and fork. Unfortunately, my parents did not have the pleasure of being the first ones to see my first achievements. I was under the care of nurses who specialised in assisting deaf children, which was a great help for me and my parents. By the age of one, not only was I walking, I'd begun to realise running was fun too. I would do this up and down the ward (so I've been told!).

I also became fascinated with another patient—a little boy who sat in his cot all day, reading books. He had no arms or legs, but was able to turn the pages with his tongue. I would often sit at his bedside and watch him.

Of course, living at the hospital had its fair share of challenges. After the operations were performed, I had a bandage covering my right eye and bandages covering both ears. These were made of hard material, feeling like a plaster cast wrapped around the top of my head. It looked like I was wearing a crash helmet that appeared to be far too big for the size of my body. My mum recalls that when I started to get tired, my head would start to flop to one side from the sheer weight of the hard bandages.

And, I had to wear these for weeks. I suppose I looked something like an alien!

When the time came to remove the plaster cast and my eye patch, the surgeons were not sure how my sight or hearing would actually turn out. That meant I'd have to stay on the ward for observation. I also furthered my development with the nurses, who taught me how to eat properly by sitting at a table along with the other children, use a knife and fork, and drink from cups.

Eye and hearing tests became normal to me, as the medical staff monitored me for any changes. I was also fitted with a brace that was strapped around my chest and tied at the back. It had pockets at the front that held two hearing devices with thick wiring. These connected to earpieces that sat in each ear. The fitted garment was very tight and uncomfortable, and felt like thick canvas material across my chest. I'd wear this for many years to come.

\*\*\*

A few months into the New Year, the nurses told me the day had finally come when I would be going home. I'd been in the hospital since September of the previous year, and had spent months before that in Queen Elizabeth Hospital, so coming home felt like a big event. In fact, I still remember it well—even to this day.

My mum and dad arrived at the ward with a present. It was a bright yellow duck that had friction wheels, and I just couldn't stop swiping the floor with the wheels and then watching it speed off along the ground on the ward, trying not to make it crash into the cots on either side. My parents watched with smiles on their faces. I wasn't the only person happy that I was going home.

For my parents, life seemed to be less hectic now that the weekly car journeys to Oxford were not happening on a regular basis. In fact, they'd only have to head out that way again for a few routine outpatient appointments.

Unfortunately, the operation on my left ear had been unsuccessful. I still cannot hear in that ear even today. But on the other hand, the right ear was a remarkable improvement. From me not being able to hear due to the ear canal not being fully formed and nerve damage within the ear, to being able to hear sounds with the use of a hearing aid was fantastic. The surgery had certainly made a difference. What level I'd be able to hear, though, was yet to be determined.

The removal of the cyst in my right eye had likewise been a successful operation, but my sight had been affected due to the scarring that had been left behind. My eyesight would not deteriorate any further, but it also would not improve either.

John Radcliffe Hospital had done what it could for me, but the journey was far from over. Further appointments to check my hearing and sight would have to be planned. The doctors told my parents that future check-up appointments with regards to my hearing could be at the Royal National Throat, Nose and Ear Hospital in London. My eyes would have to be checked at Moorfields Eye Hospital in London. Overall, it amounted to monthly appointments for any one of my conditions.

Finally, the infirmary referred me to St. Thomas' Hospital in London, where doctors could conduct further investigations into my facial deformity under the care of the oral surgery department. No one knew what that would lead to, but it was clear the work wasn't done yet.

As if this wasn't enough, my parents had to learn how to communicate with me, since my hearing was still pretty poor. They were told to make sure they faced me when they spoke, ensuring they spoke clearly enough for me to understand their words. It was another routine to adjust to, but after the past couple of long-distance months, my parents were more than ready for the challenge, if it meant having me at home.

CHAPTER 3

# "The greatest parents in the world" and "the uncertainty of what was to come."

In the midst of spending most of my first year of life in the hospital, I learnt early on that my parents loved me. They were the greatest parents in the world and gave me everything I needed and so much more. When we arrived back from the hospital, they made home a safe and secure place for me, one that I grew up loving.

I couldn't count how many times my dad would make me laugh with his jokes, and long stories that kept me amused for hours. He loved singing, belting out 'My Way' by Frank Sinatra on more than one occasion. There was never a dull moment when Dad was around. Mum was more practical, and always clever. She did all the accounting for my dad's business. She'd often hand out sweets to schoolchildren during break times or lunch, since we lived right in front of a school. I can imagine my mum must have been very popular with all the children.

As the months passed and I enjoyed the attention and kindness of my parents, I also got to know my older brother, Lee. He'd spent a lot of time at my nan and grandad's house when I'd been in hospital—and he'd definitely enjoyed obtaining some much-deserved attention and getting spoilt—but we quickly bonded. Even though I knew my conditions made his life tumultuous sometimes, especially when I had to go into the hospitals for operations or check-ups, he never resented me in any way.

But that didn't mean Lee didn't act like a stroppy child at times, especially on one occasion when he was five. He'd just started school in the building behind our house, and often played with a little boy named Kenny. Kenny would come over from time to time while his mother was at work, and my mum would keep an eye on him.

One day, Kenny and my brother were rolling a giant whiskey bottle they'd taken from our house back and forth to each other.

Mum and Dad typically used that bottle to collect spare change, but the boys thought it was great fun to roll it across the ground as hard as they could until the other boy caught it. The game ended abruptly when the bottle hit something and shattered, glass flying everywhere.

Knowing that he shouldn't have been playing with the bottle, my brother tried to pick up the coins and broken glass to hide the evidence. Within moments, he'd cut his finger and screamed for my mum.

Mum staunched the bleeding and placed the finger back into position, tightly wrapping it with bandages before rushing to the local hospital. The nurses there told her that wrapping it tightly had actually saved my brother's finger. He was very lucky there was no permanent damage.

\*\*\*

Over the years, growing up, I also got to know my extended family, including both sets of grandparents. My brother and I often got to go to my mum's parents'—our Nan and Grandad Parks—house in Stoke Newington. Our typical Saturday schedule consisted of shopping with Nan at Ridley Road Market and coming back home to catch the early-evening television in front of the fire—eating bars of Cadbury's chocolate or other loads of sweets Nan would buy, of course. Grandad would drink his tea, making sure their dog didn't knock it from the coffee table as she often did.

Nan and Grandad Parks were polar opposites, which at times entertained us. My nan, my mum's mum, was strict in her manners and sometimes very Victorian in her ways—though that never stopped her from spoiling us with all manner of sweets and treats. She set a bedtime for us and gave us each a hot-water bottle to protect us against the crisp, cold, cotton sheets and icy-cold bedroom. If we still had our lights on past our bedtime, she'd eventually call out: "Come on now, lights off. Go to sleep." Since I hated the dark, Nan would leave my door slightly open so the hallway light would shine through.

Grandad, on the other hand, loved to wind Nan up. He was a quiet man of few words, and a great builder. He was what they called a "jack of all trades"; he could turn his hand to anything, including plumbing, brickwork, electrics, and general DIY. He didn't put his talents to use when Nan often commented that she wanted the house decorated, though. He thought the house looked just fine the way it was.

My brother and I were happy with the way the house looked, too. At times, it felt like we were living in a comedy show in their little lounge, which was decorated with bulky furniture and an oversized coffee table in the middle of the room. You'd have to watch yourself when you squeezed between the fire and the armchair to get to the table and settee. Sometimes, all hell would break loose.

We'd often have little picnics on the lounge's floor, featuring sweets, tea, and biscuits in front of the fire. Picnics meant Nan would be doing her usual stressing at the mess, shoving the dog out of the room as my grandad relaxed. Other times, my brother Lee would watch *Doctor Who*, his favourite programme. The beginning of that programme scared me, and my cousin Joanne and I would always grab cushions from the settee and hide behind them whenever it came on.

Things got even more hectic when we had family meetups with my dad's parents, Nan and Grandad Skinner. All my aunts, uncles, and cousins would gather together in my grandparents' house, and there'd be plenty of food to go around. Grandad Skinner would sit back in his chair as the commotion ensued, just trying to watch his horse races on the television.

During these gatherings, we'd often watch the grown-ups play cards or bingo—my Nan's favourite game. Since my cousins were quite a bit younger than me and my brother, they would often play with the toys they had brought with them or just run around. While I sometimes joined in on their fun, I felt content to spend time with my grandparents and all the people who loved me.

Perhaps that's why being home, or at either of my grandparents' houses, gave me a unique sense of security. Their love and care fostered my growth, and I truly enjoyed the company of my family, even amid routine hospital appointments and the uncertainty of what was to come.

But as my brother and I grew, it was time to venture out from my safe little bubble and start school. When Lee began attending primary school, I began to attend a day nursery.

CHAPTER 4

# "How did you get like that? Does it hurt?"

I arrived at Nursery Ann's as a snotty-nosed, pale looking little girl. Shy and uncertain of myself, in addition to my vision and hearing problems, I didn't have much going for me when I began school life— and the constant adjustments to my "looks" didn't help.

First, I had a brace attached to my chest with hearing aids linked up to each ear. Soon, I also had to wear glasses to strengthen the muscles in my eye. I was offered a little round, pink pair of "National Health glasses", which had bendy arms on them. Although my parents were not ungrateful, they considered the NHS glasses to be very unattractive and decided to buy a nicer pair that were red in colour. They also got a second pair for me, in blue. But even that didn't help my confidence, especially as I began interacting with other children.

At the age of five, hearing aid, glasses, and all, I

began my primary education. Walking into the school corridor with my mum, I looked at the huge building and my stomach churned at the thought of being left here alone, not knowing when and if my mother would ever come back. Tears filled my eyes as my mum gave my hand a reassuring squeeze.

A lady, who must have been the teacher or teacher's aide, approached us and gave me a big smile. She gently took my hand as the sobs bubbled up in my throat, ushering me into a nearby classroom as my mum waved goodbye.

"Here's a sandpit, Shelley, see?" the lady said, leading me over to a little sandbox in the corner of the room. "This is going to be so much fun!"

As the weeks progressed, I began to settle into my new schedule. Mum bought me pure white socks that looked lovely, but they had a hard time staying up on my thin legs. I was forever pulling them up, frustrated as they continued to slip down to my ankles every minute of the day. (How I dream of having slim legs now!). She'd also spoken to my teacher about the difficulties I faced with my hearing, and they'd discussed whether I could cope well at school. "Let's just see how things go and how Shelley progresses," the teacher suggested.

So that was that. Not going to school wasn't an option,

a fact that I grew to resent as the other children made me realise just how "different" I was compared to them.

While my hearing had always been an issue, I was used to having people accommodate me by speaking directly to me like my parents did. At school, especially with the other children, it was hard to communicate. In class, I'd try very hard to hear the teacher but would often not understand what I needed to do in the lesson. That left me to pester the person next to me, asking my most common question: "What do we have to do?" If anyone asked me a question I couldn't hear or if I answered a question wrong, everyone would ridicule me by calling me stupid and thick.

As if that didn't set me apart enough, the children were even more focused on pointing out the differences in my face compared to theirs. "What's wrong with your face?" they'd ask bluntly. Or they'd come right up to me and ask: "How did you get like that? Does it hurt?" Sometimes, they'd simply state straight out: "Your face looks really funny."

When I told my mum about the invasive, hurtful questions, she simply told me to say that I'd been born that way. I followed her instructions, but I was so shy and timid that it hardly stopped the others from making a point of laughing at or making comments about my face. At times, it would get even worse. More than once, the boys ran around the playground, making silly faces and pulling their ears out, calling me "funny face" and making loud noises. The other children soon caught onto this and would join in. Other times, when we were asked to work in groups or get into teams, no one would pick me or the teacher would just push me into a random group.

No, it wasn't long before I began to feel very, very different from the other children.

Despite these difficulties, I always tried to make friends. My first friend, a girl my age named Kerryjo, somehow managed to cut through the drone of bullying and mean comments with her boisterous attitude. Her mum and mine used to chat at the infant school gates together, and we lived close to each other, which was the perfect recipe for the perfect friendship.

I felt safe with Kerryjo and followed her around like a little lost sheep, sitting by her in lessons and constantly hanging out with her outside of school. Once in a while, both of us, her mum, my mum, my nan and my brother would all go to Spain or Italy for a summer holiday as our dads worked back in England. We'd go to each other's houses daily and play with our dolls and prams, and when we got older we'd ride our bikes to the nearby park. We also both thought we were great singers, which meant playing records loudly and singing along with them to decide who was the better vocalist!

Unfortunately, even friendship couldn't protect me from the inevitable embarrassment I felt at school in front of my peers and even my teachers. Because I couldn't hear well and was constantly asking what we had to do for assignments, my reports at school often said, "Shelley is a good pupil, but very easily distracted." My mum instructed me to "always ask if you're not sure about something," but I quickly realised that if I was to spend time asking the teacher to confirm what we had to do, she wouldn't get around to teaching the rest of the class.

So, I simply avoided my embarrassment by not putting my hand up during lessons, trying my best to understand the subjects from the textbooks we read.

CHAPTER 5

# "My mouth wired shut"

At seven years of age, I had to face another operation—this time at St. Thomas' Hospital in London. While my previous surgeries were focused on my vision and hearing loss, this would be the first operation to address my underdeveloped jaw and facial reconstruction.

I was put under the care of Dr. Hovel, who specialised in treating children with facial deformities. He explained to my parents how a previous surgical procedure he had performed on a boy's foot had been successful in implanting part of the boy's rib bone into his foot to improve its growth and mobility. He planned to try a similar procedure on me for my face, where he'd take a section of one of my left rib bones, implant it into the right side of my lower jaw to increase the length of the jawbone, and hope that the bone would settle and grow in line with my natural growth.

After a number of outpatient appointments for X-rays, dental impressions and photographs, the day

Young Shelley: With my brother Lee (above), who I didn't really know in the first year of my life. We quickly bonded. He never resented me in any way.

*Shelley*

Happy Christmas: My older brother Lee was always the big protective brother most sisters or brothers would want.

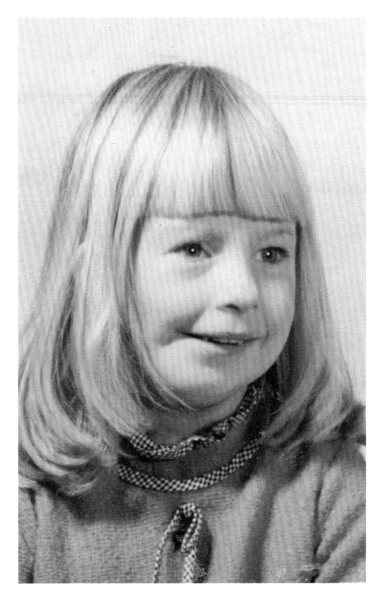

Walking into school: I looked at the huge building and my stomach
churned at the thought of being left here alone.

## Shelley

I myself had never
looked at my hair
as being beautiful;
I looked at it as my
disguise. Letting my
face show? Anything
was better than that.

# SHELLEY HULL

# Shelley

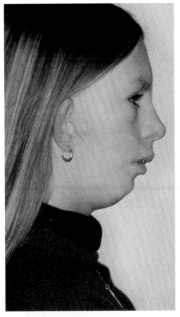 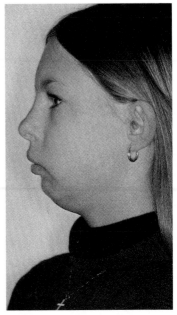

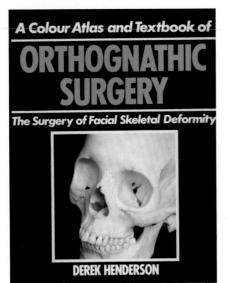

Face to face: "Oh, you didn't know? You're in the famous orthognathic book."
The surgeon got up and went to his office, bringing back a huge book for me to see.

# SHELLEY HULL

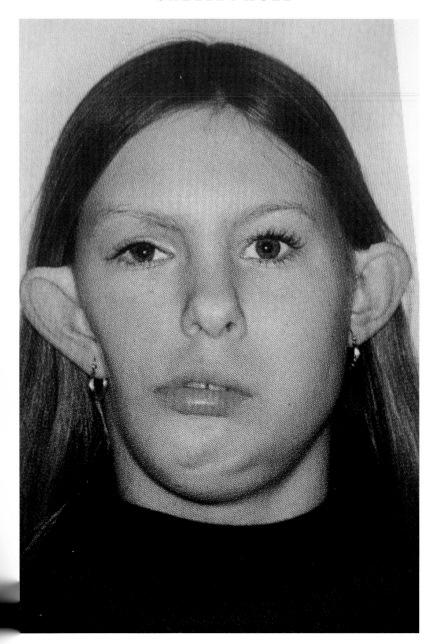

## Shelley

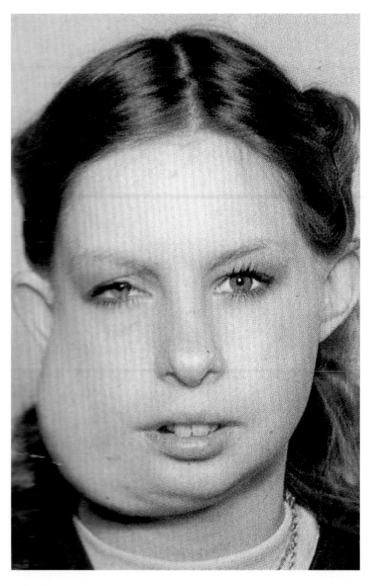

My days in the photography department: It became a natural process for me at the hospitals I attended. My hair would be pulled back with clips holding my hair away from my face.

of my operation loomed closer and closer. One of the steps was to get numerous dental impressions done on my upper and lower teeth, which I didn't enjoy at all. Basically, they put a grey, cement-like material in some metal plates and then inserted these into my mouth. After me enduring about fifteen minutes of tasting the disgusting stuff, the staff would have to take the hardened cement out of my mouth to obtain the impressions my teeth had made. On one or two occasions, this material actually pulled a tooth out of my mouth. While sometimes they used a pink, gummy substance that was easier to remove, I never forgot the awful feeling of the hard, gross-tasting cement in my mouth.

After all the impressions had been made, the medical staff made a plan for wiring my jaw shut, which would be required during and after surgery to keep my jaw completely still and to enable my jawbones to set. They made a gold-coloured casing from the impressions, and on the outside of the casing were clips so the metal wires could be tied closed together. A slight gap was left in the side of the upper casing, with just enough room for a straw to fit through, so I could have liquid food or drink.

One concern of the surgery, besides the risk of failure, was my heart murmur. My heart would beat in different rhythms and sometimes irregular beats. I would always have to be closely monitored under anaesthetic at all times, including after the surgery.

While I nervously awaited the surgery, my mum and dad reassured me that everything would be fine, as they always did. Being young, I took their word for it—but I'm sure they were even more nervous than I was.

Even though I'd been in hospital before, waking up from surgery with bandages around my chest where the rib bone had been removed, along with my jaw being wired shut, was a new experience that I didn't enjoy. The bandages around my chest were wrapped tightly, like a strapless vest that was fitted from under my armpits down to my waist. Everything was extremely well-padded, with layers of gauze and winding layers of bandages. While they weren't exceptionally uncomfortable, having my mouth wired shut was a different matter.

The surgeons had made the cut for my bone implant just under the right side of my jaw, and the bone was screwed into the existing bone. The wound had been stitched up and was covered with padded gauze, along with layers of bandages, which were eventually wrapped around my head to keep them tight. The gold casing I'd had impressions for was tied firmly together to keep my jawbones set and position them for what the surgeons referred to as the "knitting together" stage. Some of my antibiotics and pain relief came through the small gap in my casing, along with all my liquid foods. At times, I'd feel like I couldn't breathe—even though I could breathe through my nose, something about having my mouth forced shut made me panic at times.

Even more disappointing to my seven-year-old mind was the fact that I couldn't eat any solid foods for weeks, including my favourite food: biscuits (except ginger biscuits, mind you! I used to dunk them into my cup of tea, wait until they were just soft enough, and then plunge them into my mouth.) I also wasn't able to eat chips either, a close second on my favourite foods list. Instead, I could only eat Heinz baby food (though I suppose it wasn't too bad, since there were fifty-seven varieties!). I enjoyed the chocolate pudding, which to me tasted like warm chocolate custard. I also grew to appreciate Farley's Rusks along with soups, semolina, custards—really anything, as long as it was sloppy.

It was awful, watching all the other children on the ward eat their goodies that visitors would bring in, while I had my well-mushed up, liquid food. On the other hand, I did refine my skills as a ventriloquist. My mouth being wired together only allowed my lips to move, which meant I couldn't really pronounce consonants—"gottle of geer", for instance. I never did get good at jokes, but at least the operation was out of the way.

CHAPTER 6

# "The doctors had given my mum a pair of surgical pliers in case of an emergency"

The time came when I was allowed home, still with bandages covering my scars and the wires tightly tied to keep my jaws closed. My mum had to keep a careful watch over me, since I had no way to breathe except through my nose. A closed airway due to a cold or the flu could be devastating. As a precaution, the doctors had given my mum a pair of surgical pliers in case of an emergency, to be used to cut the wires to release my jaws if needed. This was only to be done in an absolute emergency, as the operation would have to be done again if my jawbone moved at all. I suppose it was like when someone breaks a bone, like their arm or leg. It has to be in plaster for some time for the bone to knit back together. While everyone had to treat me like fine china in a tea shop, my parents were more than a little pleased to have me back home. They constantly made sure I was comfortable, thankful that they could see me every day for more than a couple of hours at a time during visiting hours. Life was as normal as it could be as we waited for my bones to heal, trying to patiently count down the days until my follow-up appointments. As usual, my dad went back to working long hours, and my mum was busy at home, doing the day-to-day running of the household and keeping my dad's accounts in order.

Although my parents managed to get out some Saturday evenings, most of the time my brother and I kept them busy when they weren't working.

***

At long last, after countless outpatient appointments and X-rays, dental impressions and more for about a year, we slowly began to discover the results of Dr. Hovel's operation. Unfortunately, the news wasn't good. The bone that had been implanted had not grown or knitted together with my other bones as planned. In fact, it had actually dissolved.

Despite my age, I knew that these results

were not good—if only because of my parents' frowns. Disappointment flooded through me, and likely the many doctors who had put so much time and effort into planning for this procedure. But the results hit my parents, who had endured the stress, worry, and anxieties of the surgery and its lengthy healing process, even harder. They'd taken me to teeth impressions, X-rays, photographs, and even teeth extractions throughout the months in the hope that I'd have a chance at gaining a better quality of life. Hearing that nothing had changed—in fact, I had more scars than before and had missed school—was a harsh blow.

All this, it seemed, for nothing.

The doctors informed my mum and dad that the best course of action would be to monitor my growth and keep a check on my development. The plan was to wait until I stopped growing and try another operation once the bones in my face had fully matured. That meant I would have to wait until I was sixteen—usually the age when the facial bones stop growing—to undergo another operation. My parents were relieved at this news, taking small comfort in the fact that I wouldn't have to have major surgery again for a long while. I was, of course, to continue with my regular outpatient appointments.

Dr. Hovel was planning to retire in that time, and explained that my new doctor would be Dr. Derek Henderson, an oral surgeon who'd take care of me in the future and during my outpatient appointments. He was highly recommended by Dr. Hovel, as he had a keen interest in maxillofacial deformities. I wasn't sure what any of this meant or the impact it would have on the rest of my life, thanks to my parents putting on a brave face for me.

What their optimism did tell me was that we'd get through this, one way or another.

***

From a very young age and especially after my surgery, I got used to the photo shoots. Not the glamorous kind, of course—ones with metal instruments inserted in my mouth, pulling at each side to show my teeth, both upper jaw and lower jaw. This was always so uncomfortable. My mouth would feel so sore and the nerves in my jaws would ache, causing my lips to twitch for a while after. Other photographs were of my ears, from the front and sides. My hair would be pulled back with clips holding my hair away from my face. Then more photos of my face—again front, side to side, and even leaning my head back to show an angle from the chin up, and then the opposite downwards. That was how I spent my day in the photography department. It became a natural process for me at the hospitals I attended. There was also a similar pattern in the X-ray department. These continued for a further ten years.

As we travelled from hospital to hospital, following Dr. Henderson's treatment plan and getting photos taken, more doctors got interested in my case. Intrigued by my rare condition and eager to help treat it, they asked my mother if the student doctors working under them could meet me. These meetings also became relatively normal for me, and I never complained about having to go. They took place at an assortment of hospitals I was being treated at, including The Lister, The Westminster, The Royal Dental, and St. Bart's.

Mum would sit right outside the clinic room where a group of student doctors awaited me. I would sit down in front of a group of ten to fifteen students, who stood in a horseshoe formation with clipboards and pens in their hands. As I told my story, they stared at me with raised eyebrows and jotted down notes on the clipboards. Almost always, they informed me that my case was an unusual one—and if they didn't, I could certainly see it in their facial expressions—and they were baffled as to what had caused it. Often, they were asked to assess my condition and see what they could come up with as a learning exercise.

They were also quite blunt in asking questions, sometimes politely asking me if they could examine me. They'd have me look left, right, up, down, open my mouth, close my mouth. They used metal tools to keep my mouth open or see where the procedures had been done. The chair I sat in always swivelled every which way as they all took a turn.

I didn't really mind, because I didn't know anything different. It was normal for me to have doctors and students push and prod, examining and asking questions.

***

As I continued going about my regular schedule, post-surgery, I soon began to see changes in the scars that the operation had left me with. They began to heal really well, even though the redness took quite some time to fade into a more normal-looking colour. I always felt a tightness in the jaw when I lifted my head slightly, as the scar was in the crease just below my right jawbone. This was the same for the scar on my tummy, near my rib cage. I had to make sure my clothing did not rub against it. My mum always liked me to wear a vest, which kept clothing—especially the elastic on my knickers—away from my skin. (I must have worn very large knickers very high up on my waist, or maybe it was just the way I pulled them up… who knows?)

I also had to continue learning how to cope with my lack of hearing, and regularly attended the Royal National Throat, Nose and Ear Hospital to monitor my hearing. The audiology room was always a little square room with grey, thick material on the walls to make it extra soundproof. My mum would sit outside while I was having a hearing test. The audiologist would place what appeared to be enormous headphones over my ears. I could never get the headphones to sit properly on my head with my odd ears; trying to juggle them so they sat securely over each ear was a tiring process.

Finally, the test would begin. Once I heard any sound, I was to say yes or nod to acknowledge I had heard something. Sometimes the sounds were low and deep, sometimes they were screeching and high-pitched. Modern technology has changed that method. I still continue to have hearing tests, but there's no need for nods or a raised hand. I have a button that I press to acknowledge the sounds of the beeps.

While the tests and appointments carried on, I still had trouble with hearing at home, school, and out of the house. I had to learn how to read body language growing up, and my mum adapted well to this. She would always make sure she was looking at me when she spoke, in order for me to try and understand everything she said. I never really told her, but I'm sure she always exaggerated her sounds when speaking—especially since over the years, people have often said my mum talks quite loud. My dad was the same. Looking back, I am very grateful for how they tried so hard to communicate with me.

My brother, on the other hand, seemed to think the hearing aids that sat in my pocket held microphones in them. He'd often lean forward and shout into the little boxes, not realizing that I'd actually heard him through the earpieces in my ears. Mum would constantly correct him, saying: "Don't shout at Shelley. Just talk to her like you talk to me." It's a joke my brother and I still have today.

CHAPTER 7

# "The pressure was getting to me. Being different was the worst thing in the world"

Although my major bone graft surgery was to wait until I was sixteen, I would still face a number of surgeries to prepare me for the operation. I'd have to endure tooth extractions on numerous separate occasions, to make way for the expected growth of bone after my second major operation. At fourteen, under the advice of Dr. Henderson, I'd also go into hospital again to have my tonsils and adenoids out. This was a safety precaution that had to be done since my throat was too small for the airway pipe to be inserted—a fact that the doctors had discovered during a previous operation.

And so, while Dr. Henderson would consistently

be my primary doctor from age seven well into my late teens, my future wasn't so certain. My anticipated surgeries and conditions would extend to affect nearly every facet of my life—which meant my parents had to consider carefully where I'd go to school for the remainder of my education.

With my challenges in understanding my peers and teachers in primary school, the doctors and my parents briefly discussed whether or not I should go to a school for the deaf. My parents, having endured years of me being in and out of hospital, didn't want to send me away to live and board in a deaf school. They believed that with their help, I would settle in and cope with a mainstream school.

Over time, I grew used to my hearing aids, which helped me adapt to nursery and infant school. My parents even invited my whole class to my house on a few occasions for my birthday, which helped me fit in a bit more. In his true joker fashion, my dad would arrange all the party games, and one was especially popular with all the children. My mum and dad would hang a massive sheet up across the middle of the living room, dividing the room into two sections. Dad would hold a torch behind the sheet and each person, in turn, had to follow the lighted torch along the sheet up and down with their nose, only to be greeted with a wet sponge splatting them in the face once their nose reached the top of the sheet.

Soon, it was time to go to junior school, which set my nerves on edge. Kerryjo was still around to support me, which was nice, but I also knew that junior school took place in a separate building and on a different street from my infant school. It was also much larger, catering to all the nearby infant schools in the area.

The new stares and comments about my face were a little more bearable with the familiarity of Kerryjo at my side, and I continued to counter them with my characteristic, "I was born this way." My brother Lee, who was older than me, was also always the big protective brother most sisters or brothers would want. He constantly looked after me and sorted things out, especially if children were being horrible.

The hospital agreed that I could start to wean myself off the hearing aids, which I desperately wanted. No other child at my school wore hearing aids, and I'd dealt with people staring at my face more than enough—I wasn't going to give them more ammunition.

As a child struggling through school, hyper-conscious of whatever anyone thought, cruel words and looks had become my worst nightmare.

The pressure was getting to me. Being different was the worst thing in the world.

Without my perceived burden weighing me down, I also had to tackle my next problem: PE lessons. My heart murmur kept me from doing sporting activities at school. The doctors had advised me to stay away from physical activity, including simply running, because it would put stress on my heart. But as I grew, the murmur became very slight and my doctors gave me the go-ahead to participate, as long as I didn't overdo it. I began to enjoy playing netball, and played the position of goal shooter. That meant I must have been a good height as an eleven-year-old, though that would change when I simply stopped growing at 5"4. Not that tall, really.

I like to say that the heart murmur is the reason I'm no good at sports... even though I know that even if I wasn't born with a heart murmur, I probably still wouldn't be good at sports!

Unfortunately, after about a year, the news came about that my family was going to have to move to another town because of my dad's job. Thoughts of terror raced through my mind, one after another.

*No more Kerryjo.*

*No more friends.*

*New people. More comments.*

Despite my anxiety, I didn't complain to my parents. I knew they worked hard for our family, and I didn't want to cause any more problems in their life. Instead, I simply packed up with my brother and left, trying to muster up the courage to face my new school... and peers.

\*\*\*

Though the adjustment was difficult, I managed to make some friends at my new school. One in particular was Michelle, whose mum once accidentally caught my long hair in her sewing machine. I'd been standing too close to it as she sewed, and it got stuck. She had to cut off a chunk of my hair just to free me. There was also Ellen, who would come to my house some days while other days I'd go to hers. She always made me laugh, and was very popular in school. Sometimes she'd get told off by the teachers, but it never seemed to bother her—something I think I admired, deep down.

I began to succeed a bit more in school, taking a liking to maths lessons—especially learning the twelve times table. Every Friday was test day, and my teacher, Mr. Tanner, was my favourite. While he was very strict, I liked him because he spoke loudly. I could hear everything he was saying.

Meanwhile, my brother set to work charming his new peers, who seemed to flock to him right away. He even joined a local junior football club, and my dad helped run it. After winning a lot of medals and being friendly to pretty much everyone, he became fairly popular. Everybody wanted to be his friend.

When I reached the age of eleven, it was time to start looking at which secondary school I would be attending. My brother had already found success in his secondary school, and he didn't want to leave it. That meant we'd be going to different schools and my brother, ever my protector, wouldn't have to worry about looking after me anymore.

While I was happy for him, I dreaded changing schools and facing a new group of people completely alone.

Truth be told, I was really beginning to feel the pressure and embarrassment of how I looked. I hated my face, and all the scars from my surgery. My intended operation at age sixteen seemed like a lifetime away. I began to feel sorry for myself, constantly wondering: *Why me?*

Why was I the only one in the world who looked like this?

Why couldn't I be *normal*, like the other girls?

I didn't want to be different.

I just wanted to fit in.

CHAPTER 8

# "I liked a few boys, but no one in the class wanted to go out with the oddball, the weird-looking girl"

The first thing I noticed about secondary school was all the people. Students were everywhere—in the hallways, outside the school, in the classrooms. The second thing I noticed was the maze of classrooms and classes spread out across the building. Somehow, I managed to navigate my way through everything into my first classroom, slumping down in a chair as I waited for my French class to start. I could feel my heart beating in my ears as some of the other students in the classroom immediately began casting glances my way, whispering to each other with frowns on their faces. *Will I ever make friends?* I wondered. *How will I fit in? How am I going to cope with this?* Dread rose in my throat as another negative thought flashed through my mind. *I'll be the odd one out as always.*

"Shelley Skinner?" I hadn't realised my new teacher was standing in front of the room, taking attendance.

"Yes, sir!" I said, much too loudly, and a dozen other faces turned to look at me. I could just read the looks they gave me. *Who is she? Why does her face look like that?*

I slumped down a little more in my chair, grateful that I'd at least had the sense to sit at the back. With my hearing problems, it probably wasn't the best choice, but it made me feel more secure to be tucked out of the way.

"Hi," a voice to my right sounded, and I looked over to find a girl my age looking at me. Slowly, but surely, we started having a conversation.

A few other girls joined in, and we made small talk. They asked me a few questions, mercifully leaving my face out of the mix. "What school did you come from?" they asked, along with some other standard questions like: "Do you know anyone here at school?" For the first time that day, I felt a little better about secondary school. We managed to form a little bubble of friendliness while my teacher explained our timetable and what we should expect on a daily basis.

Suddenly, though, the lesson ended. The girls I'd made friends with were suddenly heading off to different classes, and the thought of meeting new faces at every lesson spiked my anxiety once more. With a deep breath, I walked out of the classroom to find my next class.

***

My first week passed slowly, nearly overwhelming me with all the new things I had to get used to. I had boatloads of new homework, and had to buy fancy paper to cover all my textbooks and keep them clean. One class I was already enjoying was Geography, since I was interested in learning about places. Others I found really boring and dry, and I had a hard time staying focused on the subjects.

There was also the matter of lunch and break times, where children would either merge in the playground and field to have their snacks or take refuge in the nearest school hall. Break times were about fifteen minutes, then we'd all have to rush to get to our next lesson, which didn't leave much time for socialising.

Lunch was decent—the food was, at least. But once I got through the neat, orderly line and received my choice of dish, I had to worry about finding someone to sit next to. I learnt to try and look for a friend in the queue or at one of the cafeteria tables. I couldn't bear the thought of sitting next to someone I didn't know. I knew they wouldn't want me to sit with them. That's how I felt.

\*\*\*

I passed most of my time at school alone, especially in my first year. While I did make friends with some of the girls throughout my time there, even they couldn't protect me from the other students every second of the day. I also felt that I couldn't join in on their fun at times, like when they started to talk about boys who they fancied or ones who fancied them. I watched in awe as they spoke excitedly to each other about their crushes. "So-and-so is going out with him," they'd gossip happily, or: "She has packed him in."

No boy ever liked me, of course. I liked a few, but no one in the class wanted to go out with the oddball, the weird-looking girl. I soon came to realise just how cruel boys could be when they all started calling me "Popeye" because of the way my face looked. For years and years, that name would haunt me. There was not a day that went by without someone shouting "Popeye!" at me, whether in the corridor, dining room, playing fields, or even the classroom. My dear friends would try to step in when they could, which I truly appreciated, but that didn't make the insults hurt any less.

One thing I never did was complain to my mum or dad. I'd have an occasional crying spell here or there, and I'm sure my parents knew about the bullying, but I tried not to reveal anything that happened to me at school. I didn't want them to go up to the school to defend me or complain. That would just put more of a target on my back. It wasn't normal for parents to be in touch with teachers at that time, unless it was for bad reasons like truancy or fighting.

I was in this alone, and had to deal with the pressure.

CHAPTER 9

# "I myself had never looked at my hair as being beautiful; I looked at it as my disguise"

The other students weren't the only bullies I dealt with in school; some of my worst memories also included teachers. PE days especially were awful. I always tried to be unwell and say to my mum, "I have a tummy ache," or something like that. But my mum was quite strict. "You'll be okay when you get to school," she'd say. "See how you go, and if you really feel unwell, go to the office and get them to ring me." I never did, of course.

The reason for me wanting to skip this lesson so badly was because my PE teacher always insisted I tie my hair up in an elastic band to keep it out of my face. I had long hair, and often my friends would comment and say how lovely it was, which was a really kind thing to say. I myself had never looked at my hair as being beautiful; I looked at it as my disguise. I could pull it forward around my face and hide behind it. Even then, my ears would stick out through my makeshift veil—but it was better than tying up my hair and letting my entire face show. Anything was better than that.

So, even though for safety reasons it made sense, putting my hair up was one of my worst nightmares. It exposed me, making me feel humiliated that my disfigurement was on full display for all to see and laugh at. My wonky eye, my odd, lopsided ears, a crooked face—and my scar under my jaw. I asked the teacher if I could just tuck my hair in my shirt, but she was insistent. I had to put it up.

My embarrassment increased tenfold on days when we had to go outside on the field. We would be near the boys playing football, and often had to walk or run near them. Boys would shout out to the girls and wolf-whistle at them, while the attention they gave to me was much crueller—calling me names and sharing a snigger or two amongst themselves.

Another incident occurred after my metalwork class. The metalwork classroom was an outbuilding, accessed by double swing glass doors. It was always hot in the classroom, but I enjoyed working with my hands to create something practical. That day, our task was to make a shoe horn. Once we'd finished, I headed out during break time and walked back into the school corridor to find my next class. As I walked through the doors, one of the metalwork teachers stopped me. He wasn't my teacher, but I recognised him from the classroom. He was a very tall, thin, stern-looking man. His brow furrowed as he looked down at me and sternly told me to get rid of what I was eating.

"No, s—sir… I—I'm not eating anything…," I blurted, feeling like the blood from my feet was going to burst out of the top of my head as my face burned with embarrassment.

"Are you sure?" he snapped, narrowing his eyes at me.

Tears filled my eyes as I shook my head again. "No, sir. I'm not eating…"

He perused me for a few, agonising moments, eyes lingering on the left side of my face. I knew why. That side was much fatter than my right side, which was flat and almost lopsided since it was underdeveloped. I supposed it must have looked like I was hiding some food or something inside my mouth, to someone who hadn't seen me before. The tears in my eyes threatened to spill as he asked my name and what form I was in.

"Get to your lesson," he ordered finally, and I could hardly stop myself from running fast and far away from him, already hoping I'd never see him again.

Even though I'd done nothing wrong, I still felt shame at being told off by a teacher, accused of breaking the rules simply because my face looked different from everyone else's. *Why me?* I asked myself for what seemed like the billionth time. Why couldn't I just be normal?

The only choice I had was to wait until I turned sixteen and have my second facial reconstruction surgery. Then, maybe, my life would change. It was the one hope I clung to for many years.

CHAPTER 10

# "As much as I loved my friends for standing up for me, I never really got the concept of standing up for myself"

A s awful as much of my experience in school was, I can laugh at some things. For example, during lessons, the teacher would always begin instructions about a particular lesson, informing us face to face—then they would turn around and write instructions on the blackboard. Since they weren't facing me, I could never hear the rest of the conversation. I would often nudge my friend sitting next to me and say: "What have we got to do?"

More often than not, they'd reply, "Shh—listen!" The problem was, I *was* trying to listen... but I couldn't hear! I always ended up at the end of the lesson asking the teacher for reconfirmation. This might have been avoided if I'd simply worn my hearing aids to school, but I was never going to do that and stick out even more than I already did.

***

I can imagine lots of young girls like I was have dreams of becoming a superstar in their future years, whether that meant being a model, pop singer, dancer, or having some other high-profile career. As far back as I can remember—probably the minute I started learning to talk!—my passion was singing. All day long, I would be singing at home, listening to records my parents had bought.  My mum was very keen on listening to the popular songs at the top of the charts, whereas my dad's favourite music was always the likes of Frank Sinatra, Nat King Cole, and Engelbert Humperdinck. My teen idol was Donny Osmond. His posters covered every square inch of my bedroom walls, and I must have had every single and LP that he made. I became so dedicated, I joined his fan club.

I would often play my records and sing along, recording my vocals on my tape recorder. Although I had a lot of difficulties in hearing the exact words being sung, I often improvised with my own words to the sound of the tune. Sometimes, I would ask my mum to listen to the songs and write the words down for me. But for the most part, it didn't matter to me. Behind my bedroom's closed door, surrounded by my posters and the music, I felt comfortable and protected enough to sing at the top of my lungs. It was like I was a million miles away from others' judgmental opinions. I was in my own little world.

When I'd turned ten years old, I used to watch *Junior Showtime* on TV. It was a programme that featured lots of songs and dancing, and I became determined to become a part of it. With Mum's help, I wrote a letter to the producer and sent it off. To my delight, I received a letter back asking me to attend an audition. But singing outside my little world, in front of a huge audience, petrified me. I decided to back out, not ready to leave the comfort of the little, safe world I'd created for myself. Still, the urge to share my talent with the world didn't leave me. A couple of years later, I looked through the Yellow Pages we had at home to find a recording studio in London. I rang them and asked them for some advice on how I could go about making a record. My heart sank when they began explaining the process to me.

"Obviously it makes a difference if you've got a good voice," the music producer said, not even hesitating as he added, "but of course you need to have the right appearance. Music is about creating an image."

The words hit me hard, because I felt as if I'd never be able to live up to the physical standards the music industry appeared to demand. It's amazing how things have changed now, with the rise of the Internet and openness towards all sorts of looks. But going down that route wasn't for me. I kept my love for music close to my heart, and still enjoy singing around the house—making up the words when I can't hear them!

In my teenage years, I also found some solace in fashion and makeup, like many girls my age. My mum always wore makeup—even false eyelashes—a stunning-looking lady. I spent a lot of my time experimenting with her makeup, including different eye shadows, mascaras, and every colour lipstick ever made. At the time, bright blue was in fashion. I'd practise in my bedroom and eventually came to the conclusion that makeup disguised my features, much like my hair tended to disguise my ears. Gradually, I worked my disguise down to a fine art.

I'd put more eyeshadow on my smaller, right eye, shading the colour slightly to make it look bigger and to cover up the fact that my upper lid cut across the corner of my eye (doctors referred to it as being like a cleft palate of the eyelid). I would also apply eyeliner to the bottom of my eyes under the lashes to enhance the lower part of my eyes, never putting it on the top so it would not highlight the difference too much. My mascara went just on the outer side of the lashes. On my right eye, I didn't have many lashes in the corner, so I had to make sure I only applied the mascara to the outer lashes and lower lashes. I would apply the blusher to my cheeks and not on the cheekbones, as my cheekbones were not symmetrical. And I loved lipstick—all the colours.

In a way, makeup made me feel more comfortable in my skin.

I began to love makeup so much that when the girls started to break the school rules in 2nd Form and lightly dust their faces with powders, mascara, and eyeshadows during the day, I longed to give it a try. Finally, I worked up the courage to do it one day and wore a full face of makeup to school. My teacher immediately called me from the back of the class and told me off for wearing it, making it quite clear that I needed to go into the toilets and wash it off.

She was right, a rule was a rule. But I'd really thought it would make me look better, and had wanted to fit in as usual. Unfortunately, my plan had backfired.

I never wore makeup to school again, not wanting to face the embarrassment of being scolded in front of the class.

Still, I found other ways to change my looks and keep up with the latest fashions in the Third Year, when a new hairstyle emerged as a trend. In the past, I'd wanted to cut my hair shorter like the other girls, but I hadn't thought the cut—then called the Purdey Cut—would be flattering on me, with its super-short style exposing the ears. My ears were already nicknamed "Dumbo", so I definitely didn't want to draw more attention to them—even if Joanna Lumley (Purdey from the popular TV show, *The Avengers*), had the same cut.

But I just couldn't resist it. This latest hairstyle was too tempting to pass up, and I finally plucked up the courage to go for it. My long hair—so long that I could actually sit on it—was finally cut to shoulder level. The style, called the Page Boy, was a cut where the length of the hair was shaped around the face. I didn't want to have my hair shaped around my face for obvious reasons, so I tweaked the style a bit and had it cut to just above my shoulders with the same length all around to the front. Always thinking about my disguise, I also had a side parting, with the long length dropping down the right side of my face.

It was everything I'd hoped for and more. After having long, quite limp hair for most of my life, my new haircut felt bouncy and smooth when I turned my head from side to side. My friends also made me feel good by complimenting me on how nice my hair looked. I was over the moon. I felt more comfortable than I ever had in my skin, and gained maybe a shred of confidence from the experience.

My ecstasy was short-lived, however. The first day back at school after having it cut, the horrible comments arrived—mostly from the boys, as usual. "Look!" they yelled, pointing and jeering. "She's got a lampshade for her bulb!"

Quite why they seemed to think my abnormalities made my head look like a lightbulb, with my new haircut as its shade, I had no idea. But they did.

\*\*\*

Every single mean word, every bully, got to me in one way or another. The children were clever; they never shouted comments when teachers were present, only when other children were around. They thought it would make them stand out and look big, to pick on me in front of the others. I would take their insults quietly, even as my face turned bright red and gave away my embarrassment. Sometimes, a friend would shout back and say: "Leave her alone—don't be horrible. She can't help the way she looks!"

As much as I loved my friends for standing up for me, I never really got the concept of standing up for myself. I never went to the school office or in fact told teachers that I was getting called names. I was fearful of causing a fuss and wasn't comfortable discussing my disfigurement with anyone. Why would I be? No one else looked the way I did. I just wanted to keep my head down, do my work, and hurry through my school years as quick as I could. And even though being called names daily was very hard to bear at times, I didn't see any other option.

Looking back now and having taught in schools myself, I only wish that the teachers had been more understanding. But, unfortunately, we've only just begun to tailor schools to accommodate and assist all kinds of children with different needs.

Thankfully, we are now teaching our children to include and understand a person who is different from them.

The bravest thing I could have done back then would have been to stand up in front of the class and explain how and why I looked the way I did, and why

I had difficulty hearing. Most of the children—with the exception of a few—would probably have understood, and I might have felt more comfortable. Sadly, I didn't have the confidence to do that at the time.

Secondary school never got easier, though I did learn to cope with things a bit better once I'd made some friends. And what good friends they were: Kerry, Valerie and Anne all supported me and stood up for me and would become lifelong friends. Not that I felt I could look forward to the future with much confidence.

Thankfully, the school Fifth Year came with the promise of preparing for my CSE's and O-level exams and getting out of school for good. Most of my coursework was up to date and it was coming up to Christmas 1978, which meant I'd start my mock exams after the holidays.

An unremarkable Christmas came and went and, before I knew it, 1979 was upon us. This was to be a great year for me. I was sixteen, and Dr. Henderson and the team of doctors who'd been following my case had begun talking to us about my next operation. While I didn't know the details yet, all I could do was dream about how it would fix all my problems. I was going to have a normal face. No more bullying, no

more shyness. The moment I had been waiting for all
these years had finally come.

CHAPTER 11

# "My prayers had finally been answered. The date for the surgery had been set"

I came home from school one day and my mum told me there was a letter waiting for me. I scrambled to open it, tearing through the paper and scanning the contents.

My lottery had arrived—my winnings. My prayers had finally been answered. The date for the surgery had been set.

My parents made it a point to talk to me about the surgery, making sure I still wanted to go through with it. My dad told me that if I didn't want to endure another operation and recovery process, it didn't matter to him. I'd always be his little girl. My mum felt the same way, but I was adamant. I didn't think about the what-ifs or whys, or whether it would work for me—or even whether or not it would be a long recovery.

I wanted to be able to walk down the street without people staring and wondering if I had been in an accident. I wanted to be able to look in a mirror without cringing, and have my photo taken without glancing to one side to hide my underdeveloped face. I wanted to be able to wear my hair the way I wanted— even cut short.

The letter stated that the operation was set to occur in February. Mum and Dad sat me down and talked to me again, trying to thrash out the details as my mind whirred with happy thoughts and dreams come true.

"Do you want to wait a few months, so you can finish your exams first?" Mum asked.

*No way.* I had waited years, and I didn't want to wait any longer. School could wait.

My parents finally wrote a letter to the school, explaining that I'd be going into hospital in February and they didn't know if I'd be returning to school or not—at least for a year, anyway. That was fine with me. School was the last thing on my mind, and I planned to cross that bridge when I came to it.

***

The next couple of weeks were crazy ones, where my mum would drive me to St. Thomas' Hospital to have a multitude of tests for the operations. These included the standard X-rays, impressions, blood tests, and others—basically routine for me by now. When the day came for me to be admitted, a couple of days before the operation was due to start, I had a few final tests and my mum and I sat down with Dr. Henderson to discuss what the surgery would actually entail.

"The surgery's going to take about eleven hours," he explained. "We're going to take some of Shelley's hipbone and place it into her right jaw, through the same incision point as the previous operation. The scar's going to be a bit bigger than last time, going up to about your earlobe," he said, helping my parents visualise what this would mean.

In addition to the bone graft, both my cheekbones would be cut and moved into a more symmetrical position, including my upper jaw. Dr. Henderson would complete this task by making incisions inside my mouth, above my upper teeth. To hold everything in place, I'd have a large metal cage screwed into my eyebrow bones, with a bar coming down in front of my nose and joined in my mouth, connected to a metal casing.

I listened to him silently, drinking in his every word. None of this information deterred me, because I trusted my life in his hands. He'd been with me from the start, slowly making the necessary recommendations to prepare me for this surgery, for years as my primary doctor and source of wisdom. I'd grown up under his care and knew he'd do his best to help me complete this journey. If there was any doctor who was going to succeed in treating my condition, it was going to be Dr. Henderson.

My mum, on the other hand, was extremely worried. I could see it on her face, and hear it in the questions she asked. That made me more concerned than anything else, but I wouldn't be swayed. I had to try this.

After our meeting, I was checked into the ward with all my things. Familiar with hospital stays thanks to all my previous surgeries, I always packed so much stuff to take with me—in a way, it was like a holiday. I'd always enjoyed craft-making and sewing, and took some of these activities with me, along with nail polishes, books, and other things. I was also used to my parents only being able to see me during visiting times, though that part never really got easier.

Once I was all ready with the paperwork, Sister Riley, the matron of the ward, greeted me. She was in charge of what would become like a second home to me: Wardroper Ward. She would also become a lovely, caring friend, sort of like a strict aunt. Later, I'd come to know the other nurses and orderlies, who would often refer to me as "Young Shelley".

Sister Riley showed me where everything was on the ward—toilets, the dayroom, bathrooms. After I'd placed my things in my room and spoken to her, I had to go down to the oral surgery department to have my metal casement braces sealed onto my upper and lower teeth in preparation for my major surgery.

That preparatory work on my teeth, of course, wasn't so pleasant. The liquid inside was like a glue that actually cemented the gold casing onto my own teeth, and it tasted revolting. The disgusting liquid always managed to trickle down my throat as the casing was pushed up onto my teeth and would ooze out at the edges. Metal wires protruded on the outer side of the casing, so a pink, plasticine-type gel was placed over them to stop them from rubbing the inside of my mouth and lips. During the surgery, my mouth would be wired together, the wires tight so the casing would close my jaws tightly together.

By the time I got completely settled in, it was about 7.30 p.m., and Mum had to leave and drive back home. I was OK, but again I noticed how worriedly my mum was acting. I gave her a tight hug and reassured her, trying to relax in my new room and show her I was OK. My dad later telephoned the ward and asked to speak to me, which he would do every night and every time I was in hospital. As he had explained before, he told me that he'd love me no matter what, and he was sorry he couldn't be there for me on the ward. Unfortunately, he had such a fear of heights due to a tragic accident years ago that he couldn't come up to see me on the seventh floor—but hearing his voice was all I needed. I let him know I was fine and that I'd look after everyone in the ward, as one of the more experienced patients.

The next day, Sister Riley nominated me to help out on the ward by serving drinks to the other patients. I loved doing this, feeling like a grown-up as I chatted with other patients and offered them their evening drinks. Obviously, after surgery, it'd be a while before I could resume these evening duties.

I met so many interesting people who'd travelled to London for their surgery.

In many ways, I felt more comfortable in the hospital than I did anywhere else. Here, it was okay to be different—we were all here to get "fixed", and we all accepted each other's situations. So what if I looked different here? It was a change of pace, I felt comfortable and perhaps part of me felt I belonged, but it didn't stop me wanting desperately to go ahead with the surgery. I wondered what it would feel like once I had a normal face. Would the hospital still hold this magic charm for me?

## CHAPTER 12

# "I could see a difference straight away.
# My chin seemed to look more in the middle of my face, where it should be"

Getting the news of my operation, prepping for it, and even the surgery itself flew by in a blur, and the next thing I knew I was back on the ward following surgery and waking up with drains hooked up to my face and hip. They dripped into glass bottles hanging over the side of the bed, collecting excess blood.

"Your mum and dad have phoned so many times to see if you were out of theatre yet," Sister Riley told me as I groggily looked at her.

Dazed as I was from all the pain, tablets and

antibiotics they had me on—not to mention the fact that part of my hipbone was now missing—I knew I wouldn't be getting out of bed any time soon. After about a day or so, I was allowed to sip water through a straw that slipped through the small gap in the gold casing in my mouth. This was to be how I drank and ate—only liquids for twelve long weeks. Regular salt dabbing of my lips and the skin around where the metal poles were inserted into my head became a four-hourly routine for the nurses. Vaseline was always applied to stop the frame screwed into my eyebrow bones from scabbing around the edges. These processes, and many others, became the norm for me as the days continued to drag on.

Although I don't remember much pain, I do remember the uncomfortable feelings I felt. I couldn't talk, could barely move, and even something as simple as drinking some water took effort. After about five or six days the drains were removed, which gave me a bit more mobility than before. But the large frame in my head was still something that I needed to get used to, along with the many bandages I had and drips I was still on.

For the next four weeks, the highlight of my day was at 2.30 p.m., when I would look out of the ward window to find Westminster Bridge and Big Ben.

Below, I'd be able to see my mum walking across the bridge to come and visit me, and more than anything her company kept me going. I always hated when she had to leave at the end of visiting hours, but in the evening I was allowed to use the phone. The nurses would wheel it over to me and my dad would call. I would try to speak to him as best I could, but since my mouth was wired shut he did most of the talking.

"You're one brave girl," he'd always say, and I could hear him grin on the other end of the line. "Don't worry. You'll soon be coming home and we'll be here, waiting for you."

His voice always cheered me up, even as I sat alone in my hospital bed, unable to move or talk. I'd always try my hardest not to cry and let him know how uncomfortable I felt, as I knew he would worry.

After days confined to my ward, I was allowed to get out of bed and be pushed in a wheelchair, which was lovely. I could now go downstairs to the canteen and meet my dad, brother, nan and my friends. It was such a nice feeling to come off the ward for a while.

By now, I was also getting used to having the frame on my head. In fact, Sister Riley tied paper flowers on each corner on the top to glam it up. I might have laughed at the spectacle we made of it, but it was difficult to laugh, sigh, or even smile, as the metal

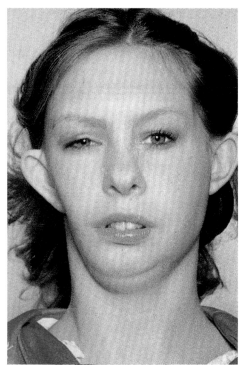

More pictures from surgeon Dr. Derek Henderson's textbook: His remarkable work changed my life. He had watched me grow from a timid young girl into a survivor and had been there through some of my darkest times.

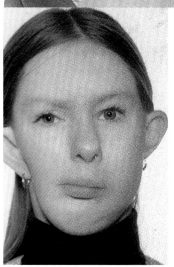

# Shelley

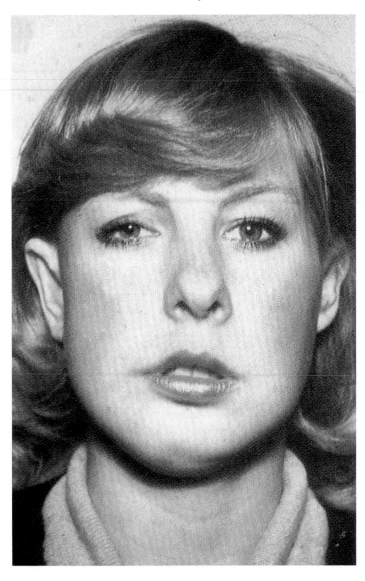

The largely successful years of surgery: My chin seemed to look more in the middle of my face, where it should be. I still had a long way to go, but I was pleased.

# SHELLEY HULL

Growing confidence:
I was still concious of how I looked, but instead of staying quiet when people bluntly asked what had happened to my face, or if I had toothache, I'd simply say: "Oh no, I had facial surgery."
If only I'd discovered that simple tactic sooner, when children were bullying me at school!

Below: With young patient Tamsin, who was undergoing similar surgery to that which I had endured for so long.

*Shelley*

October 1985: My special wedding day. Left: with brother Lee and Mum and Dad. Above: With my Dad on the way to the ceremony. He loved joking and singing. There was never a dull moment when Dad was around.

## Shelley

Right now, I feel a million years away from all my facial surgeries. Despite the irreversable nerve damage and hearing loss, I'd say it's a small price to pay for so much gained.

Below: My incredibly loving parents with the ever-supportive Lee.

# SHELLEY HULL

Hoping to inspire others:
Here I am with Becky
Hyams from Aylesbury,
Buckinghamshire, at the
2015 Goldenhar convention
in Glasgow. Becky's father
Steven Hyams is executive
committee member and
treasurer for the Goldenhar
charity

# Shelley

Talking through my experiences at Goldenhar: My name was at the bottom of the list. *12.30 p.m. Speaker - Shelley.* Seeing it written on paper filled my stomach with butterflies. But when a lump formed in my throat and tears came to my eyes it wasn't for sorrow or sadness. *Those children in the audience looked like I once did.*

rods inserted in my eyebrows would make my skin start stinging. My cheekbones also felt very tight and uncomfortable when I moved my face in the slightest.

At the end of the second week in hospital, I was allowed to start walking—carefully, so I didn't put too much pressure on my hip. I found it really hard at first, as my hip was very sore every time I put pressure on my legs. Luckily, pain relief and antibiotics helped. I had to have these by intravenous injections, since I couldn't take the tablets orally. The recovery process continued.

Every day, I managed to feel better and stronger. I began to apply the Vaseline and mouth cream myself, and used salted mouthwash to clean the stitches—which would eventually dissolve—in my mouth.

When we finally hit the four-week mark, I was allowed to go home, with instructions to come back to the clinic on a weekly basis. It felt wonderful being able to go home, but I was also nervous. I still had a large dressing on my hip and jaw, and the big frame screwed to my head. I found it hard to sleep in my normal bed, as the corners of the frame would point into the pillow and tug—so the best way to sleep was to lie on my back, slightly propped up.

Soon, though, the familiarity of home and

family made me more comfortable. While I found it hard to cope with the frame and the annoyance of having my mouth being wired shut, it felt good to be in my own room again. Still, I had never seen anyone with a frame like I had before, not even in hospital. I did not want to go out at all. Once, I went with my mum to our local shops, and again people stared and asked my mum what had happened.

Hating the thought of looking even worse, like some type of alien, I tried my best to keep the faith that everything would turn out OK. I couldn't—*wouldn't*—think that the operation was a waste, not until I knew the results. The only thing I could do was avoid people other than my family and the hospital staff, and wait.

After twelve weeks, it was time for the frame to be removed. Unscrewing the rods from the mouth connector was fine, but from the eyebrows—not so much. It didn't really hurt, but I could feel the sensation of the twisting rods vibrating through my eyebrow bones. It was a strange, horrid feeling. The following week, the wires were untied from the metal casing over my mouth.

"Open your mouth now, Shelley," the consultant said.

I must have opened it a fraction of a millimetre, but it felt like I had my mouth wide open. Having my jaw shut for so long made the movement feel weird, like I'd broken a bone and had it set for decades.

Although I was still very swollen and puffy, I could see a difference straight away. Even my nose looked different. My chin seemed to look more in the middle of my face, where it should be. I still had a long way to go, but I was pleased. After so long, I was finally seeing some improvement.

Two weeks later, the casing was removed, piece by piece. I felt like all my teeth were going to come out with the cement, since when I was seven some actually had. But, teeth intact, the casing came off and I was sent home to continue healing. It took a couple of months for the swelling to start settling down, and by then the movement in my jaw was much better. I managed to apply some makeup, which made me feel like I was getting back to my normal routine.

School was coming to an end, and my Head Teacher visited me at home, bringing me a collection of "get well" cards. We discussed the possibilities of returning to school in the sixth form, but I had made up my mind. School was not a good place for me, and if I didn't have to go back, I really didn't want to go.

CHAPTER 13

# "She ended up in a bed next to mine— my mum, 'the nurse'"

My Head Teacher and I continued to come up with a plan, since I didn't want to go back to school. I was also to have more surgery in the future, which continued to be my priority. But while my body healed and the doctors prepped for the next operation, I'd have to find something to do. My Head Teacher recommended that I enrol at my local Careers Office for advice on finding a job. The Careers Advisor was very helpful and suggested, since I was going to have more surgery, I enrol on a course that would fit in around my future surgery dates. I ended up on a Manpower Course for secretarial studies.

Feeling lucky to be considered for the course, I couldn't wait to get started. It wasn't a fully-paid role, but I did get a small wage. The position was at Ford Motor Company, and I had a great manager who helped me learn the skills I needed to become a good secretary. I worked hard to learn audio typing, which was one of my greatest achievements. While it was a struggle, I managed to get through it by turning the volume up full blast to compensate for my hearing difficulties.

And although I never learnt shorthand, I could listen to Dictaphone tapes and transcribe them with very few mistakes. This gave me a boost of confidence I'd never known in school.

I was working, and people respected me. It was a big, wonderful change.

In fact, I enjoyed it so much that even though the job was only to be for six months, they managed to extend my time—even allowing me to have surgery in-between. Everyone was so understanding and accommodating—for once, I felt special and valued by people other than my family.

My job also kept me preoccupied from getting too impatient about my surgery progress. The swelling still hadn't gone down, and while I could see some changes, I still longed for a normal face. Through all of my insistence, I'd somehow missed everyone telling me that this would be a long recovery process. Even despite this, my dream had arrived and I was buying it at whatever cost I had to pay.

The next bill came when I was seventeen, due

to go back to the hospital for yet another big operation. This time, I would have plastic surgery work as well as more hip bone implanted into my face. One consolation was that I wouldn't have to have the large, uncomfortable frame I'd endured during the previous surgery, since my cheekbones were not being moved. All the internal movement of my bones was done, so it was time to insert some padding into my right side.

Dr. Henderson and his team would do the surgery under microscope, since nerves, muscle, and tissue were to be taken from the left hip and placed in the right side of my face. Again, the scar would be opened on the right side of my face, just under my chin—only this time, the scar was to be made wider in order to insert all the bits under the skin.

***

Surgery day arrived, and Sister Riley was there to greet me as always and took me around the ward, introducing me to the patients as one of her "regular residents". She was a lovely sister—very strict in nature and firm, but very kind. Every morning, she walked around the ward with her cheerful, "Good morning, ladies, time to rise and shine!" Then she'd open all the windows for fresh air. Sister Riley never took any nonsense, but encouraged patients to feel good and get well with her uplifting spirit and character. She was a lady I would always admire.

This time, the operation was filmed for medical purposes at St. Thomas' Hospital, since I was one of the first in the country to have this sort of procedure done. The oral surgery team and plastic surgery team worked together to insert a bulk of fat and skin tissue in the right side of my face.

Waking up from surgery that day, I was shocked to see the amount of dressing covering most of my lower body and the top of my thigh. I had no idea how big the scar on my hip would be, but when the nurses removed the dressing to clean the wound, I realised it was much bigger than I had anticipated. I would later find out that it travelled from the top part of my left leg, through my groin, over my left hip, and around to my back. The reason for this was to avoid very important blood vessels in my legs and groin. I supposed it was a small price to pay for my dream of a normal face.

The scar wasn't the only surprise that greeted me when I woke up. When my mum came to the ward to visit me at 2.30 p.m., from a distance she thought I had something like a large bandage attached to my face. In reality, the side of my face was actually resting on my shoulder—it was *that* big. Apparently, the doctors had inserted much more fat and tissue than I needed because the skin would shrink as it healed and distort the size. They wanted to put as much in as possible so they'd only have to remove the excess, instead of having to put more in at a future date.

So, in addition to the large dressing at my hip, I had stitches from the corner of my right cheek bone down through the middle of my face to my lip, with pieces of gauze poking out at intervals of stitches. These stitches were also underneath my face, and there were internal stitches as well. Bandages covered the newly-opened scar under my jawbone, and again drains were in my neck and hip, getting rid of the excess blood.

Once more, I couldn't remember being in pain—just discomfort. At least I could talk within a few days following surgery, and could even eat sloppy food that didn't require much chewing.

After a few days in hospital, I began feeling unwell and the colour of the skin on my face was changing to a bluey-looking colour. An infection had started and a collection of blood and fluid was starting to form. The consultants had to come to the ward to drain the fluid with syringes. Due to this, I had to stay longer in hospital.

Once things settled down a bit, the nurse informed me that I'd have the drains in my neck and hip taken out. My mum was there with me, and watched as the nurse pulled the screen around us. I prepared myself for the unpleasant process of getting the drains pulled out, looking forward to getting some freedom. Unfortunately, since the drains were stitched into my skin so they didn't move, the nurse would have to take extra care to get them out.

"Ah, the lights aren't bright enough in here for me to see the stitches," the nurse mumbled after examining me for a moment. "Give me a minute while I get another nurse to hold the torch."

"I'll hold it," Mum volunteered, standing up. She'd been in the hospital so much with me over the years that she'd become interested in being a nurse. Since she'd never had the time to pursue that career, she decided to at least help out where she could.

So there I was, laid flat on my back on the bed, looking up at the ceiling hoping the nurse would get this over and done with. I could see the torch's light shining on the curtains, then the ceiling, then the curtains again. *What's going on?* I wondered, not able to move or talk yet. The nurse was close to my neck, removing stitches to get the drain out, but she didn't have any light.

I was totally unaware, but my mum had watched the nurse take the stitches out, then pull the drain out of my neck. She hadn't realised how far the drain was in my skin and had begun to feel queasy… then fainted! She'd pulled at the curtains as she'd fallen, and a nurse came running in and caught her from slamming into the floor.

She ended up in a bed next to mine—my mum, "the nurse".

About half an hour later, I found out what had actually happened—much to Mum's embarrassment! Thankfully, she was fine and the nurses were happy for her to go home at the end of visiting time.

***

Life carried on in the hospital, and I was finally discharged from the ward to return to the clinic on a weekly basis as an outpatient. Eventually, they removed all the stitches from my face and hip, and I started to recuperate. Over the next few months, all the swelling and bruising began to settle; however, the skin did not shrink much at all. I had what appeared to be a very large cheek. The colour of my skin—about a three-inch strip held in place by stitches across the front of my cheek—had also visibly turned yellow.

That, of course, meant more surgery—which none of us were too pleased about. The first couple of operations, to debulk my right cheek, worked fairly well. After each reduction, the yellow strip began to get less and less, leaving me with just a slight discolouration. Eventually, I felt that even that slight blemish blended into my normal skin.

In some subsequent operations, they inserted Proplast, a type of plastic bone, into my face to level out my jaw. Unfortunately, this became infected for no apparent reason. Despite many antibiotics, most of the synthetic bones had to be removed.

The removal of the Proplast was frustrating for me, since I'd noticed how the bones had made my chin more symmetrical and given me a better profile. But with infections and abscesses, I also understood that they needed to be removed. My perfect chin profile had to go.

After all the reductions on the right side of my face, the doctors sat me down and explained that although I had endured countless surgeries to correct the symmetry of both sides of my face, it would be completely impossible to ensure that my face would be totally symmetrical. My childhood dream of having a perfectly "normal" face would forever be out of my reach—but somehow, it didn't matter so much anymore. Deep down, in fact, I think I always knew that would be the case.

Even though I'd never achieve perfect symmetry—and although I still had some way to go—I couldn't be anything but immeasurably grateful for the end result.

I was still conscious of how I looked—but not necessarily the same type of self-consciousness I'd felt in my youth. Instead of staying quiet when people bluntly asked what had happened to my face, or if I had a toothache, I'd simply say: "Oh no, I had facial surgery." That was that, and I found that most people didn't press me for more. If only I'd discovered that tactic sooner, when children were bullying me at school.

## CHAPTER 14

# "For the first time in my life, I began looking in the mirror and liking what I saw"

Now in my eighteenth year, and having completed my secretarial course at Ford, I applied for a secretarial job in a high street bank. I ended up loving the years I worked there, enjoying the company of some very nice people. The combination of my jobs gave me the confidence I needed to pass my driving test at seventeen, so when I turned eighteen my parents bought me my first car. It was a lovely feeling, to be able to drive to my friend's houses and pick them up and go out. Sometimes, I would drive to work near London or park at the station to catch the train.

For the first time in my life, I began looking in the mirror and liking what I saw. My face was more symmetrical, even with the missing Proplast, and my scars were healing. I could wear as much makeup as I wanted, and even started going out to clubs with my friends and taking a couple of holidays here and there. It was as if a new life had just begun for me, and surgeries were on the back burner. I felt like a completely different person, and though my physical changes had helped, I also realised it was more than that. I'd finally gained the confidence to just be me, even if at times I was still uncomfortable in my own skin.

My new-found independence led me out on a couple of dates, something I had never experienced while at school. Even though I only had one or two boyfriends, it was so nice to have the excitement of someone liking me and wanting to go out with me.

In 1984, I met my husband-to-be. We fell in love and enjoyed each other's company. I obviously told him all about my operations, and although he could see something had been done, he was not concerned about how I looked and reassured me that I was beautiful in his eyes. In October 1985, we had a lovely wedding with all our family and friends there to celebrate our special day.

As my marriage began over the next few years, the major surgeries and their implications finally ended when all the Proplast was removed after so many infections. Although my journey never really ended, I decided to forego further surgeries for the time being and focus on my new life with my husband. I'd still have to go to regular check-ups at the hospital for the usual tests to make sure all was well, but now I could focus on raising a family.

Enjoying life was fantastic and extremely busy having three sons under five, keeping up with all the chores of running a home and fitting in after-school clubs. It is true what people say, that children grow up so quickly. The time flew past as the boys grew and participated in rugby. Most of the matches were at weekends. It was such good fun—mind you, I do not miss the muddy boots and having to wash their kits every time they played. Evenings were taken up with the boys and their school homework.

Finally, when they started secondary school, I managed to have a bit more free time and I started to do evening classes. I'd always enjoyed crafts, so I enrolled in so many courses over the years—Curtain-Making, Faberge Egg-Making, Handmade Ceramics, Hairdressing, Floristry, Reflexology, and even Dog Grooming. I enjoyed each and every one. Once the boys were older, I went back to work part-time locally to help with the family income.

***

Despite my happy family, the impact on my life caused by my abnormalities never really ended. In my early twenties, I began to struggle even more with my hearing and decided to go back to wearing a hearing aid. I really needed it, as I was struggling to hear the boys at home and on the telephone. It was not long before my hearing started getting worse. After seeing consultants at the Royal National Throat, Nose and Ear Hospital in London, it was confirmed that my hearing was deteriorating due to the nerve damage and the deformity of the ear canal.

Having no hearing in my left ear and only a small amount of hearing in my right ear with a hearing aid, I made a decision to learn British Sign Language. I enrolled in my local college and passed Levels One and Two. A couple of years later, I even became a teacher of BSL at our local Adult College on a part-time basis.

To my surprise, I found a passion for teaching that I hadn't discovered before. I'd struggled very hard at school myself, both with my hearing and having a hard time absorbing too much information. That made me want to make sure my students could fully understand what I was saying and delivering. I would turn my lessons into visual activity programmes so that everyone was involved and participated.

I enjoyed teaching so much that, years later, I applied for a teaching role at my local Fire Authority. This was a massive challenge for me, but I really wanted to try. In the interview, it was agreed that I would teach in small groups due to my hearing difficulties. I would be able to lip read to help me communicate with the group. I completed my teaching qualification and my role was to deliver Fire Safety Awareness in schools across the county. I did this for quite some years.

My manager at the Fire Authority was an exceptional boss, Barry Davis, who believed in me and put me forward for many courses and skills sessions, including basic counselling skills for junior firesetters (young people who start fires). Although I had not achieved academically at school, I felt proud of what I achieved in my later years. As the saying goes, you are never too old to learn a new skill.

The demand for teaching these programmes was high, but my hearing was deteriorating further, it was becoming a problem to carry on teaching. I felt it was time to move on to pastures new. I'm now manager at my local St. Luke's Hospice shop raising money for charity and absolutely love it. I work with wonderful volunteers, exchanging stories and having a few laughs during the workday.

And who knows what my next role will be?

My boys, now men, are all grown up and working and living their lives. I still wonder where the time has gone. My dad, my rock, has since passed away, and never a day goes by without me thinking about him. I do see my mum, who lives near me. We meet on a very regular basis, and she is keeping very well. We often all go out to lunch with my brother and both families.

***

In my forties, I turned my attention back to finishing the surgery on my face. While the results of my surgeries had been phenomenal from where we'd started, I was still unhappy with the bulk of fat on the right side of my face. The easiest option at the time to get rid of it was to have liposuction. I wrote to Dr. Henderson in France, hoping he was still operating or could refer me to someone who could do the operation. After so many surgeries, I knew that I'd have to have a specialist carry out the operation.

Dr. Henderson was pleased to hear from me, and to learn that I had a grown-up family. He explained that as I got older, the right side of my face would not age with the left side due to the implants of muscles, fat, and tissues. He also confirmed that I needed to see a specialist, but he himself was retired. Within a week, he had the name of someone else I could see in London. A few weeks later, I had an appointment at The Royal London Hospital.

It was like old times, seeing the oral surgery team. They greeted me and spoke highly of Dr. Henderson, then sat down to take notes, stare, and ask questions about my condition. In a funny way, they made me feel like a bit of a celebrity. I thought it was all in my head until one of the surgeons said: "Ah, this is the famous Shelley Skinner! This is the lady who is in the book!"

I'd been Shelley Hull for years now, and hearing my maiden name made me freeze. *Famous? Book?* "Did you say a book?"

He raised his eyebrows. "Oh, you didn't know? You're in the famous orthognathic surgery book."

I couldn't help but gape at him. After all these years, I'd never known I was in a book. The surgeon got up and went to his office, bringing back a huge book for me to see. My eyes scanned the pages, drawn to my medical pictures. I was listed among many other people all over the world with medical abnormalities, surrounded by their stories and my own. The book had been written by Derek Henderson and D.E. Poswillo. It was called *A Colour Atlas and Textbook of Orthognathic Surgery: The Surgery of Facial Skeletal Deformity.*

It's hard to describe how I felt, having my entire medical journey in a book for the entire world to see. It was strange, seeing it reduced to a few sentences and some pictures when I'd lived through every agonizing comment, moment, and situation. It just showed where I'd begun and how I'd progressed, making me realise just how far I'd come to achieve my dream of being normal. The photo of the shy, innocent little girl staring out at me on the left was a far cry from the confident woman on the right.

As I processed all this, the surgeons and I agreed that I'd have liposuction to reduce the bulk of tissue in my cheek, so nothing from my previous surgery would be affected.

CHAPTER 15

# "For all those years, I thought I was the only one with this condition... I was always the odd one out. A freak"

After learning that Dr. Henderson had passed away in 2013, and feeling determined to write my story, I had my son James research medical professionals who'd been in the oral surgery department at St. Thomas' Hospital around the time I'd been there. We came across a surgeon, Dr. David Koppel, who'd trained there at around the same date and times, so I decided to email him, hoping to gain some insight into whether he remembered me or my case at all.

To my surprise, I received an email back. I had explained my case to him and that I was in the book

(*A Colour Atlas and Textbook of Orthognathic Surgery: The Surgery of Facial Skeletal Deformity*), and he did remember me. He asked me to send a recent picture to see the difference the surgeries had made. I also shared the sad news with him that Dr. Henderson had died, of which he'd been unaware as well. I wrote that Dr. Henderson and the surgeries had changed my life, and how I was going to write a book detailing the adversities I'd faced growing up. He agreed it would be a great story to tell.

We kept communicating through email, and one day he asked for permission to share my case history with his students. Of course, I was only too pleased to be of help to any student, and replied with my confirmation. Dr. Koppel also mentioned a seminar he'd be attending, and asked if I'd like to talk a little bit about my story there.

The seminar, he explained, was to take place in Glasgow in Scotland. It would be hosting a number of other professionals in the medical field who would also be delivering their lectures. Families who were facing similar medical journeys were to attend as well.

I was thrilled to share my story and speak about writing my book. I rang my mum up and told her that we'd be taking a trip to Glasgow.

\*\*\*

When Mum and I arrived at the hotel and checked in, a woman from the seminar gave us a friendly greeting. She also invited us to a gala dinner later that evening. We then ventured out to learn more about what the seminar really entailed—since all I knew was that it was a family weekend with a medical seminar on Sunday morning.

The front desk gave us an itinerary of the seminar, detailing the talks planned for the following morning. My name was right at the bottom of the list. *12.30 p.m. Speaker – Shelley.* Seeing it written on paper filled my stomach with butterflies. It was all so official. Professors and doctors would speak first, and then I'd take the stage.

We unpacked our things in the hotel room and went downstairs to the reception area to have a coffee. While we were sitting enjoying our coffee, we saw some of the seminar families sitting in small clusters on the sofas in the lounge area of the hotel. We couldn't help but notice that some of the children sitting with their families had abnormalities.

A lump formed in my throat and tears came to my eyes. It wasn't for sorrow or sadness, though. *Those children look like me,* I thought, stepping back in time into the shoes of that little girl from the pages of the old text book. I had never seen so many children who resembled the way I'd looked. We'd never even been aware of anyone who looked like me, except for a young girl in Cornwall who'd been one of Dr. Henderson's patients. Even then, we'd only heard about her when she was just beginning her surgery.

I exchanged a look with my mum, who was also clearly emotional. She knew what I had gone through as a child, and was just as awestruck as me to see so many children with the same condition. We watched as they played and ran around, having so much fun with all the other children.

*For all those years, I thought I was the only one with this condition,* I thought, dabbing at my eyes. *I was always the odd one out. A freak.*

Yet here I was in Scotland, with children who looked like me. But they were laughing, playing, having fun. They were not different; they were not odd.

They were beautiful.

It was all new to me. All these years, there were children I never knew being born with the same condition or similar conditions to what I had. I was not the only one; I *am* not the only one. I felt the love towards these beautiful children that my family had always had for me.

Why had I hated myself as a child? Why hadn't I seen what my parents could see, what my brother could see?

I couldn't stop smiling as warmth filled my heart. I wanted to get up and talk to them, but I didn't really know what to say. The families didn't know who I was, but I wanted to know more. I was overwhelmed with emotions.

We decided to freshen up in our room and then head down to the function hall, where the gala dinner night was in full swing. We were ushered to our seats in the dining room, where music was playing. The atmosphere was electric, and everyone looked smartly dressed. We sat at a large round table with about ten other seats, one of many that surrounded the dancefloor.

As the night wore on, we got to know the families and children sitting all around us. I spoke to the people sitting next to me, wondering if they knew why I was there. We also got chatting with the rest of the group, enjoying the entertainment of the evening.

As the gala drew to a close, my mum and I ventured back to our hotel room.

But I couldn't sleep.

I sat up all night, thinking about what I was going to say.

Meeting the children and their families only made the situation worse. I wanted to inspire them, to tell the parents that their children would get through treatment because I had.

But why would someone like me talk about something like that? I was no one special. And I was no different from those children.

CHAPTER 16

# "*Just introduce me as Shelley*, I said, trying not to let my voice tremble with nervousness"

The following morning came too quickly for my liking. I was up and ready early. In fact, very early, as I went down to the reception area to access the hotel's small computer room. I'd noticed that the itinerary sheet for the seminar had the heading "Goldenhar UK". I wanted to Google them and find out more about the group I'd be delivering my talk to.

I was under the impression that I was simply going to talk to a group of family members and some medical professionals who were attending the seminar. But in fact, it was Goldenhar UK's family weekend event, and there'd be plenty of medical professionals there who specialised in Goldenhar syndrome, a condition much like my own, caused by the genetic makeup of the patient. Goldenhar UK was a charity for families affected by abnormalities caused by this syndrome.

My mum came down and joined me for a coffee before we made our way up to the seminar room. It was beginning to fill up with the attending families. Some of the children had gone off for the morning to an amusement park, and the little ones were playing in a room along the corridor.

While the children were occupied, the seminar could take place. The oral surgery team was going to deliver their talk before me, and I'd be the last one to speak. A few minutes before the start, I was informed that the oral surgery team was outside in the corridor and wanted to meet me before the talks started. It was lovely to meet the team, and they advised me that Dr. David Koppel, the surgeon who had invited me to the seminar, would unfortunately not be attending due to family commitments—but they would be delivering the talk. They asked if they could show me their PowerPoint presentation.

I was quite honoured that they wanted my approval, but shocked that I hadn't even been aware that their talk was all about me. They had photos and information about all about my surgeries that they would be talking about. I hadn't been expecting that, and the added pressure made my nerves tingle again. *What am I going to say to this group?*

I kept to the back of the hall with my mum as the talks started, which meant I couldn't hear what they were saying very well. Not that it mattered; my entire mind was panicking at the thought of the team talking about my surgeries and what I would say afterwards. I suddenly didn't want to tell them all the challenges I'd faced, afraid that I'd make the families overwhelmed, sad, or angry for their children. I needed to rethink.

Halfway through the seminar, there was a short break for coffee or water for about fifteen minutes. With a deep breath, I told my mum that I was going to move to the front of the hall and sit with the oral surgery team. She just nodded, as shocked as I was about the purpose of this whole conference and my involvement in it.

Nearing the front of the hall I met Alan Holmes, who'd sorted the equipment out and had been introducing the speakers. He came up to me and quietly asked how I would like to be introduced.

"Just introduce me as Shelley," I said, trying not to let my voice tremble with nervousness. "I'll explain who I am and why I'm here."

He gave me a thumbs-up. "Okay, that's fine."

The room went quiet when the oral surgery team took the front of the room, starting to deliver their talk. They started off by explaining my background, how this talk would be about a patient who was born with a severe case of Hemifacial microsomia, contracted from German measles. I continued to watch as the slides of the PowerPoint flicked through the talking points, feeling as if I was watching them perform surgery on someone else—even though all the information was about me. It was like I was learning about another patient.

Each slide showed a diagram, then came the photos. I had never had anyone explain my surgery to me the way they did to that entire room full of people. It was mesmerising—quite unreal, really. Tears were filling my eyes as I relived the experiences in some strange, detached way. Maybe it was because I'd struggled for so long to get my "normal" face. Maybe it was because of all the setbacks. All I knew was that I was about to cry my eyes out. I had to pinch my leg to distract myself.

The families, in turn, were putting their hands up, one by one asking all sorts of questions about different stages of the surgeries. It was so strange, hearing them talk about me. After what seemed like a long time, the presentation came to a close. The selection of photos—*my* photos—stayed on the screen. The audience applauded the team as they had with the other speakers.

Alan came to the front of the room and gave me a grin as he introduced me. "Now it's time for our last speaker for today. Please give a warm welcome to Shelley!"

*Oh my God.* It was time.

\*\*\*

My hands were sweating, my heart was pounding. I could almost feel the blood rushing through my body to congeal in my face, which was turning redder by the second. *What am I going to talk about?*

I could practically hear all their thoughts, the families who'd come to the seminar seeking answers and information. *Shelley? Who is this lady? What organisation is she from? Is she is a doctor?*

I clenched my hands into fists, focusing on my breathing as I made my way to the front of the room. *Come on, Shelley. You can do this. You've spoken to audiences before when you taught.* But this was so different from all of that. I wasn't delivering sign language, or a fire escape plan.

I was talking about myself.

Somehow, some way, the words came forward. "Thank you for allowing me to come along to your family weekend, and to be part of this wonderful charity," I began, fiddling with the crib sheet in my hand. "I feel honoured to be here."

Silence, and lots of it. I took a deep breath and continued.

"These talks have been interesting and informative, haven't they?" I pointed to the photos behind me on the screen. "What did you think about the patient the team was talking about? Did you find that interesting?"

Some audience members nodded their heads, mouthing the word "yes". I gave them a soft smile.

"Well, actually, the person in the photos is me."

Mouths dropped open. Slowly, almost infinitely slowly, the audience began clapping for me. The applause increased and grew until the entire room was acknowledging what I'd just said.

At that moment, I knew exactly what to say. I just had to talk from the heart, to let them know that what they were going through was a tough road, but that getting through the hardships was more than possible. I gave them a brief insight into how I'd found life difficult when I was a young girl, and that how I'd thought there was no one else with the same condition. I explained my operations and my feelings about wanting my chance at a normal life because of the bullies at school, and how hard it was when my mum would have to leave when hospital visiting hours ended.

Most of all, I gave gratitude to all the surgeons who'd contributed in making my face and changing my life. Their support and the love of my family was what had kept me changing and growing.

"I kept strong and did my best to get through it all," I said, trying to meet every person's eyes for a second. "And now I'm in the process of writing my story. I never knew about Goldenhar syndrome, and I never imagined that children were still being born with the same condition as I was. But how fantastic is it that your children have other children to talk to and share their stories or worries with? Even you, as parents, can talk with each other, support each other."

I could see my mum at the back, dabbing tears from her eyes. I couldn't imagine where I'd have been without her and my dad, and all the family who had helped me conquer my hardships with their endless and unconditional love. "It's something my parents never had," I continued.

At the end of my talk, countless people began asking me questions and wanting to see my photographs. Talking about myself and my struggles was something I would never have dreamed of doing before the thought of writing my story or going to the seminar. To be able to share my experiences with others, to inspire them to stay strong in the face of any challenge or roadblock—it was more than I could have hoped for.

So, I reassured my newfound friends that medical knowledge had improved so much since my operations, and that it'd be easier for their children to get facial reconstructive surgery. I also learned that Proplast was no longer being used for implants anymore due to recurrent infections.

After the presentation, I was asked by the committee if I would like to be a Patron for Goldenhar UK. I am now honoured to be just that.

At the end of it all, after all the questions had been asked, I thanked everyone for allowing me to share my story. I'd gained more than they would ever realise from the experience.

I felt like I had come home.

# Shelley Today

*In spite of the hugely-uplifting end to Shelley's story, and the largely successful catalogue of operations she endured, her struggle to lead anywhere near a normal life continues today.*

*Here, as a postscript to her story, Shelley sets out the difficulties she still confronts on a daily basis and her determination to inspire and help as many people as possible born with Goldenhar syndrome.*

Right now, I feel a million years away from all my facial surgeries. This makes it easy to speak positively about something that happened so long ago, my own personal "lottery win", as I call it. But with every triumph comes complications. With any facial reconstructive surgery—and, probably, any surgery in general—there are always risks. Sometimes, things don't always go as planned. While my life is better, I'd be lying if I said it was perfect (whose is?). That's just the reality of what I went through. That said, I still believe that the potential results outweighed the risks, without question.

During one of my surgeries, for example, one of my facial nerves was damaged. This left me with a numb feeling on the right side of my cheek, including my bottom lip, which still has some trouble moving. The only time this is an inconvenience is when I have my usual trip to the dentist. Since I'm unable to lower my bottom lip, I have to hold it down with my fingers. Oh, and once in a while I'll get a crumb or something stuck to my numb cheek—so I have to rely on someone to (hopefully!) inform me. But it's not like I'm going to become an actress or an opera singer, so I'd say it's a small price to pay for so much gained.

A little more invasive is my hearing difficulty, which has deteriorated considerably. I've had countless ear infections over the past few years— probably a result of wearing my hearing aid for so long. While antibiotics can handle the damage, it's never long until the next infection comes along. Of course, not being able to hear has its advantages. Like when my husband informs me in the morning how bad the weather has been during the night and how strong the wind was. I never get disturbed. We have a running joke that if he were ever to be choking or having a bad turn in the night, he couldn't rely on me to help him.

My hearing aid is also a source of humour for me, since it often whistles and emits high-pitched feedback from the sound coming into it. I'm so used to this noise that it's only when I see people stop in their tracks and look up in the air with a confused look on their face that I realise my hearing aid is chirping. It gets worse when I use the phone. People often say: "What's that noise? Can you hear that?"

"No," I say, even though I know full well it's my hearing aid, because I've dealt with this for years. "It must be a bad line," I chuckle. Sometimes, it's just easier to bluff than give a lengthy explanation that leads to unnecessary conversations (thank goodness for texts and emails).

It's not all fun and games—but you learn to cope. Working as a teacher presented a challenge to my hearing issues throughout the years. When teaching, I'd often be getting ready to start my lesson when my hearing aid would beep in my ear and then shut off as its battery died. At first, a feeling of panic and isolation threatened to overcome me in the dead quiet. As a result, I made a back-up plan to get around this issue. I'd keep calm and ask the students to look at their textbooks or get into groups and discuss the lesson, then I'd walk back to my table and secretly replace the hearing aid battery. Eventually, I'd just replace the battery every Monday morning so it wouldn't happen again.

Less worrying, but more frequent, were

hearing problems at home, working as a mum to raise my boys. They'd be upstairs in their bedroom, usually on their PlayStation or Xbox, and would call down to ask me something—probably how much longer dinner was going to be or something along those lines. But all I'd ever hear was, "Mum… blah blah blah." That was it. I'd call up to them, "Come down! I can't hear you!" But, in typical adolescent fashion, they'd simply call down their request even louder: "MUM… BLAH BLAH BLAH." Of course, their shouting only made it harder to understand their words, since it distorted what they were saying even more. I had to constantly encourage them to face me when they were talking so I could lip read—a lesson I emphasised when I was teaching British Sign Language and Lip Reading.

There is a possibility I will get a hearing implant in the future, though it's something I'm still undecided about. I have to carefully consider that I only have one ear that has a small amount of hearing, with the help of a hearing aid. If future surgery were to be unsuccessful, there'd be a chance I'd lose my hearing completely.

Despite all these challenges I've faced with my hearing, I can't help but feel joyful.

Yes, my struggles still continue. Yes, I've had my fair share of difficult times. And yes, the challenges will never stop. But the scars are on my face and body, not in my heart.

***

I truly hope my story has given you some sort of comfort, inspiration, or perhaps even just something to relate to in your own journey. I also hope that in writing this book, I've not discriminated against or upset any person. As a patron of Goldenhar UK, I've seen children with similar facial conditions as mine. While I felt the way I did about my looks as a child, I can honestly say that I've never looked at others and felt that way about them. Every single child I've spoken to and worked with is beautiful, inside and out, as are the families who support them. I too was beautiful before my surgeries; the only "ugly" or unattractive feature about me was the negative self-doubt I harboured for so many years.

With my new face, I slowly began to dig myself out of that self-defeating cycle. Now, I am totally and completely grateful for all my operations. Every single step of the way has been worthwhile, and I have no regrets.

I still very much continue my support as a patron for Goldenhar UK and the good work they provide for families who have children with Goldenhar syndrome, which is an umbrella term for a wide range of bone abnormalities affecting the face, ears, eyes, and sometimes the vertebrae. To this day, this condition has been proven not to be genetic.

\*\*\*

To every single child and family facing this condition, have hope. Take it from someone who's lived through it. And perhaps I'll see you at the next Goldenhar convention.

THE END

# Goldenhar

Anyone wishing to find out more about Goldenhar syndrome or the Goldenhar UK charity can visit the website at www.goldenhar.org.uk

Some of the information appearing on the voluntarily-run organisation's website is reproduced below:

Goldenhar syndrome was identified in 1952 by Dr. Maurice Goldenhar (hence the name), an ophthalmologist, who wrote a number of articles about facial problems that tend to occur together. Often, in hospitals, it is referred to as Hemifacial microsomia (or Complex hemifacial microsomia).

No one yet knows why Goldenhar syndrome happens and doctors will call it "sporadic" (unknown cause). Children with Goldenhar syndrome are usually of normal intelligence and live normal life spans. We do know that a baby's face develops during the 8th to 12th week of pregnancy by several types of tissue growing together and meeting, at the same time, to form facial features. The tissues that become the face and jaw start separate from the upper part of the face.

In Goldenhar syndrome, something goes wrong with this meeting. It is not yet known why or how.

## Some common problems:

Small, missing or misshapen ears; skin tags (usually in front of the ear); mouth opening larger on one side (Macpostoma); underdevelopment of the muscles of the face (Hypoplasia); spinal vertebrae fused, missing or not formed on one side (Hemivertebrae); ribs misshapen on one side; eyes—dermoid cyst over the eye, Anophthalmia (missing eye); middle ear abnormalities—nearly all of the children have hearing loss on the abnormal side; cleft lip and or palate; breathing difficulties—some of the children with Goldenhar have required a tracheostomy soon after birth; feeding problems—some of the children have had difficulty swallowing and required tube feeding; internal problems such as kidney or heart (heart problems are less common but, occasionally, are found with this syndrome).

## General comments about Goldenhar syndrome/Hemifacial microsomia:

The main features of this condition are the unilateral underdevelopment of one ear (which may even not be present) associated with underdevelopment of the jaw and cheek on the same side of the face. When this is the only problem, it is normally referred to as Hemifacial microsomia, but when associated with other abnormalities, particularly of the vertebrae (hemivertebrae or underdeveloped vertebrae, usually in the neck) it is referred to as Goldenhar syndrome. It is likely, however, that these are two ends of the same spectrum of the same condition. The muscles of the affected side of the face are underdeveloped and there are often skin tags or pits in front of the ear, or in a line between the ear and the corner of the mouth.

There are often abnormalities of the middle ear and the ear canal may be completely absent and deafness (unilateral) is extremely common. There are also eye abnormalities including dermoid and notches in the lids, squints and occasionally small eyes. Children with the Goldenhar end of the spectrum may have a variety of heart problems. A variety of kidney abnormalities may also be present. There are a number of other, rarer congenital abnormalities that may occur. Most individuals with Goldenhar syndrome are of normal intelligence, although learning difficulties can occur in about 13 per cent of cases. These are usually language problems as a result of deafness. There may also be speech and swallowing problems.

Many babies with Goldenhar syndrome have poor weight gain in the first year or two of life. Diagnosis of Goldenhar syndrome is made clinically and no DNA abnormality has been identified. Various environmental causes have been suggested but not proven. Early identification and treatment of deafness is important and speech therapy is often necessary. Help may be required with managing feeding problems and encouraging weight gain in early infancy.

Any associated abnormalities such as congenital heart problems may need appropriate treatment. Plastic surgeons are now able to improve the growth of the face, particularly the jaw, through the use of bone distraction techniques (this is a device which is able to artificially lengthen the jaw bone). Children with Goldenhar syndrome may also need ongoing orthodontic treatment.

# About the Author

Born in East London in 1962, Shelley Hull now lives on Canvey Island in Essex with her husband, Ian, and their West Highland Terrier Molly. She has three grown-up sons, James, Ashley and Mitchell and both her mother, Helen, and brother Lee each live close by in the same part of Essex. Since writing her very personal and inspiring story, Shelley has developed an increasing need to talk about her various disabilities and encourage others to overcome the difficulties dealing with facial disfigurement. If you would like to contact Shelley, please email Hornet Books at info@hornetbooks.com

*Shelley* is also available as an ebook